TRUE CRIME FILES

24 DISTURBING TRUE CRIME STORIES OF MURDER, MYSTERY, AND MADNESS

SCOTT MATTHEWS

The true mystery of the world is the visible, not the invisible.

— Oscar Wilde

CONTENTS

INTRODUCTION

Every society is built on a fragile foundation of trust. We trust that our neighbors are who they say they are, that our leaders act in our interest, and that the world follows a predictable logic. But what happens when that trust is systematically dismantled? In *True Crime Files: 24 Disturbing True Crime Stories of Murder, Mystery, and Madness,* we step into the fractures where that foundation has crumbled, revealing a reality that is as fascinating as it is fearsome.

The cases ahead represent a global map of human transgression. This journey takes us from the unsettling discovery of a skull hidden in a child's toy in China to the high-pressure world of international deception, including Canada's infamous Busang Mirage. We aren't just looking at the act of crime but at the terrifying evolution of it. You will witness the psychological grip of the Gloriavale Christian Community, the cold-blooded calculations of the Lahori Psycho, and the lingering, taunting silence of the Jazz Murders.

While some stories explore the brutal finality of violence, others delve into the "madness" of the mind and the "mystery" of the unknown. We examine the chilling complexities of a family turned on itself in the Colt Clan case and the intellectual battle of a cipher that successfully defied the FBI's greatest minds. These are the accounts that challenge our understanding of morality—where cults sign contracts in blood and "princes" build empires on nothing but lies and audacity.

As you navigate these twenty-four files, you will find that the most disturbing monsters aren't always found in the shadows; sometimes, they are hiding in plain sight, protected by a badge, a religious robe, or a charming smile. The cases are real, the victims are many, and the truth is waiting to be uncovered.

Step inside, but be warned: once you see the world through these files, you can never look at it the same way again.

1

THE PLUSH THAT HID A SKULL

In 1999, Hong Kong police entered a Granville Road apartment after a teenage witness led them there. The flat was jarringly decorated floor-to-ceiling with Hello Kitty motifs — curtains, bedsheets, and a cluster of oversized plush toys.

Among those toys, officers found the most crucial piece of evidence: a large Hello Kitty mermaid doll with a human skull sewn inside. The remains were identified as Fan Man-yi.

Fan Man-yi's story is about how the spaces of pleasure and profit, drugs and sex, and the lure of easy money can intersect with organized crime to create an arena where a person can be stripped of their protections, their freedom, and finally their life.

Before the apartment and the mermaid doll, before the drug binges and the debt that spiraled out of control, there was a child who had been left behind. Fan Man-yi was abandoned in childhood and grew up in an orphanage until age fifteen, when the age limit forced her out. With no adoption and no home waiting, she was suddenly on her own. Homelessness came quickly. Addiction soon followed. To survive, she entered prostitution, working brothels to earn money for food and, increasingly, to feed a dependence that never stopped asking for more.

In her early twenties, she secured work as a dancer at the Empress Karaoke nightclub. There she met a client who would become her husband: a fellow drug user whose presence in her life did not halt her habits, and rather enabled them. They married in 1996 but it wasn't a happy marriage — he abused her. But despite the abuse, the couple stayed together long enough to have two sons. Even neighbors got used to the sounds of the children crying, and the adults arguing through the night. She lived in survival mode, with strain always present in the background.

By early 1997, the marriage couldn't halt the economic reality of her life. Fan returned to prostitution, working at the Romance Villa in Kowloon. It was there that she met a man whose name would become inseparable from her own in everything that followed.

Chan Man-lok was thirty-four, a wealthy figure with social pull and connections. He inhabited a world where crystal meth (ice) moved alongside money and sex. He was a dealer and a pimp, tied to the triads, and he had a circle of younger men orbiting him. For a woman in Fan's position, his presence promised cash and drugs in quantity. He paid her for long all-night sessions, supplied ice, and pulled her into the comfort of a circle that at first didn't feel like a trap.

Once she was inside that circle, the balances shifted. Comfort shaded into familiarity and soon enough, familiarity into vulnerability. In the hierarchy Chan maintained, there were underlings to do his bidding and women to supply sex and money. He was not someone to be messed with, or even associate with safely. Yet, in a moment that would become the hinge of the story, Fan did exactly that.

During a binge, Fan stole Chan's wallet. About $4,000 in cash changed hands. In ordinary street crime, it was a simple theft — money taken to feed a habit and buy dinner. Inside Chan's hierarchy, it was something else entirely: an affront that cost him face and challenged his control. The money mattered, but the insult mattered more. From that moment, the "debt" stopped being a balance to repay and became a pretext to punish.

Fan agreed to repay the $4,000 from her work but Chan refused the straightforward return of principal and demanded $10,000 in interest. She said she would need time. On the surface, it sounded conciliatory; to

Chan, it only sharpened the trespass. This was less about cash than audacity — less about the loss of money than the loss of face.

When the money didn't arrive on Chan's timetable, discipline gave way to punishment. The "debt" stopped functioning as a balance sheet and became the instrument that justified whatever came next.

In March 1999, Chan gave the order. Two of his men abducted Fan and brought her to his apartment on Granville Road. It was large, five bedrooms, decorated in Hello Kitty paraphernalia — curtains and sheets, wall décor and plush toys. The cuteness stood in absolute contrast to what would happen there. The plan, as he framed it, was straightforward: he would force her to work until she paid back the debt. The reality was that he kept moving the line. The interest kept climbing. The goalposts were never fixed. She could not reach a point where the debt was satisfied because satisfaction wasn't the point.

When the money did not appease him, punishment began. Control slid into violence and the cycle fed on itself. Beatings left her too injured to work, and her inability to work was treated as defiance that brought more beatings. The tempo matched the meth binges, with longer nights, thinner inhibitions, and spikes in irritability, impulsivity, and aggression. This was not a sudden outburst but a systematic abuse. The debt gave the pretext, the drug gave the fuel, and the group's shared indifference normalized it until laughing at her pain felt, to them, like part of the night's routine.

The core group that held Fan captive formed around Chan. There was Chan himself. There was Leung Wai-lun, a subordinate described as nineteen or twenty-one years old. There was twenty-six-years-old Leung Ching-cho. And then there was a fourteen-year-old girl known as Ah Fong, an alias for her real name. She had been groomed by Chan, described as the girlfriend of one of the underlings but also likely one of Chan's prostitutes. Young as she was, she joined in. She laughed. She invented new cruelties. She was part of the dynamic that normalized the harm and spread it around the room.

What they did to Fan was sustained, malicious, and relentless. They restrained her and beat her with whatever was at hand. There was sexual violence. They forced degrading acts and used heat and irritants to worsen her injuries. On one day, she was kicked in the head fifty times. When her legs and feet were already damaged, they struck them again to keep her from healing. They poured sauces and oils on her and turned the abuse into a cruel game, ordering her to smile and say she liked it, then threatening worse if she did not.

The humiliation kept escalating. They urinated on her and punished her when she gagged. Ah Fong forced further degrading acts meant to break her will. They wrapped her in electrical wire, hoisted her from a ceiling hook, and left her hanging through the night. Over time they stopped feeding her. The fluids they forced upon her became, grotesquely, the only intake her body received. Clients turned away from a woman so wounded she could barely stand. The men watched television, played video games, and treated her suffering as filler for hours that might otherwise have been dull. She drifted in and out of consciousness on the floor of her torturers while her husband and children waited somewhere else in the city, not knowing where she was or whether she would return.

One night, the group went out drinking. They tied Fan and left her on the bathroom floor, locking the door behind them. On April 15, 1999, after about a month of unspeakable torment, Fan died on the bathroom floor, alone and in pain. When they returned, Ah Fong went to use the bathroom and found the body. The men argued, first about what had caused her death, then about what to do next. Some believed she had overdosed, a conclusion that fit their assumptions about her drug use. Others did not settle on a single explanation. In practical terms, the argument paused nothing. They left the apartment to play arcade games indifferent to her death, and later returned to sleep, the body still behind the bathroom door.

The following day, high again, Chan gave the instruction that would turn the apartment from a scene of torture into a site of desecration. "She must be destroyed," he said. They carried her to the bathtub and dismembered her body to smaller parts that could be handled and moved, to more manageable parts. Decay and smell drove their next decisions. They boiled the parts on the stove. Chan woke Ah Fong up and sent her to put a bag of viscera into hot water to tamp down the odor. At the same time, Leong Xing Cho was boiling the head and called Ah Fong over to look.

She said she was scared and did not want to, but he told her to pretend she was watching TV. She took a quick peek and agreed it looked like something from a horror movie.

By then the process had dragged on for ten hours, and the group was getting hungry. As they tended to the pot and stirred from time to time, they started cooking noodles on the next burner. They used one spoon for both, alternating between the noodle pot and the other pot.

By the time their meal was over, the head was nothing but bones, and the skull was sewn into the head of a Hello Kitty plush — specifically a mermaid doll. Why that choice was made is not clear, and in a sense, the absence of a coherent reason is part of the horror. The object, already present among many cute objects in the apartment, became a container for what they had done. They kept other bits, a tooth and some organs, for no reason that has held up to telling. Most of the rest they disposed of in the building's garbage.

For a month, nothing happened. The flat stayed quiet. The men went on. The mermaid doll remained. Then Ah Fong walked into a police station in May and told officers she was being haunted by a ghost. It is a strange entry point into a homicide investigation, but it was the words she chose and the way she described the figure that made officers listen. The ghost, she said, had been tied with electrical wire and murdered. The haunting could have been dismissed as a teenager's nightmares, a story told to stir attention or sympathy. The details were too sharp for easy dismissal. She admitted that she had played a role in the death.

Officers followed her to the apartment. Inside, she pointed to the Hello Kitty mermaid doll. There, investigators found the skull. The rest of the flat held the residue of what the script describes: the refrigerator, the pots, the objects that, when arranged together, made the story legible in terrible clarity.

Police arrested the group and brought them to trial. The case turned on the ordinary questions of guilt and responsibility and also on the extraordinary atmosphere of cruelty that the testimony captured. Ah Fong took the deal offered. She testified against the others in exchange for immunity. She told the court she had been Chan's girlfriend, perhaps also his prostitute. When asked why they had done what they did, she said she thought it was for fun. She said she needed to speak to placate Fan's ghost, to unburden the guilt, to stop the haunting that pressed on her. Her testimony was not coy. She described the acts, the laughter, the games. The courtroom heard every detail.

The trial ran for six months. Material evidence came in as exhibits: the refrigerator where parts had been kept, the pots used in the cooking, the skull. The odor reached beyond the front rows. Psychiatrists examined the men and described them to the court as without remorse. The lack of a clean forensic path to cause of death made one part of the case unusually difficult. Given the state of the remains, the court could not assert a definite mechanism. The injuries alone could explain it; an overdose could also be consistent. Jurors were left to decide whether the defendants had killed with intent or whether they had caused death without the mental element that elevates homicide to murder.

In the end, the jury convicted them of manslaughter. They accepted that the men had caused Fan's death. They could not agree that intent had been proven beyond reasonable doubt. The guilty verdict was thus constrained, and yet the sentencing judge refused to minimize what had happened.

In December 2000, Justice Peter Nguyen sentenced the three men to life imprisonment with eligibility for parole after twenty years. His words carried a stark judgment on conduct that, in his view, stood apart. In recent years, he said, "Hong Kong's courts had not encountered such cruelty, depravity, callousness, brutality, violence, or viciousness. The public deserved protection from men like these."

In another jurisdiction, across the border in mainland China, executions might have followed swiftly. Hong Kong had no death penalty. Life with parole eligibility was the law's shape of permanent censure.

Outside the courtroom, Fan's husband spoke. Life sentences felt like a measure of justice, something he could assent to. He did not pretend that any sentence could repair what had been done. He said the words that anyone in his position might say when the formalities are over and the cameras go away: how can I ever forget.

Ah Fong, who had been fourteen when the events unfolded, walked away from criminal charges and into foster care. Her current whereabouts and the arc of her life after the case remain unknown.

The men appealed in 2003 but the sentences stood. Years passed. The apartment at thirty-one Granville Road was demolished in September 2012. The site, washed of its past in brick and glass, was rebuilt as a hotel in 2016, a place for travelers in a district that constantly remakes itself. By some dark irony, the precise location of the murder now houses a restaurant, a place designed for families and friends and the brief pleasures of a meal. In 2014, the skull that had been sewn into the doll's head — the only part of Fan's body that remained in official custody — was returned to her family. They had it cremated.

Time moved on inside prisons as well. A twenty-one parole horizon arrived in 2020. Leung Ching-cho was released in April 2014 after a court accepted that the evidence against him was insufficient, a post-conviction turn that pulled him out much earlier than the life sentence implied. He returned to the city, and not long afterward, he returned to the police's attention. In January 2022, employed as a waiter, he groped a ten-year-old girl's chest. A court later sentenced him to twelve months' imprisonment for that offense. But the status of the rest is unknown to the public.

The city's reaction mixed disbelief with fascination. Hong Kong's identity as a safe, modern city produced a cognitive dissonance with the facts. The trial's duration, the youth of the girl who took immunity, the way the men joked and cooked and stirred and ate — each detail stacked until the stack formed a portrait that felt both singular and instructive. The case moved quickly into culture. Films told the story in sensational terms. *Human Pork Chop* is a title that reflects the sensationalists' urge to make atrocities sound like jokes. *There's a Secret in My Soup* is a title that makes the mundane domestic sphere complicit in the act. Abroad, the case appeared in fictionalized form in an episode of *Bones*, an American drama series, showing that the story had crossed borders the way urban legends do, carried more by image than by nuance.

When the trial ended, the city did not forget. On Fan's birthday, people gather for a candlelight vigil in the center of Hong Kong to remember a woman whose life had been narrowed by abandonment and poverty long before her captors took her. The ritual is small compared with the spectacle of the trial, but it is truer to what memory should do. It takes a name that otherwise might be lost to the icon and places it in light. It separates the woman from the plush toy. It turns a story of degradation into, at least for an evening, a story of recognition and care.

2

THE DAY MONA DIDN'T COME HOME

On Saturday, May 31, 1975 — the first day of New Zealand's Queen's Birthday long weekend — eighteen-year-old Mona Elizabeth Blades left Hamilton intending to hitchhike home to Hastings. It was a last-minute plan. She had not told her parents she was coming because she wanted to surprise the family and bring color to an ordinary milestone: a first birthday for her nephew, marked by a small gift of tumbling plastic blocks. By Monday she was not back in Hamilton. On Tuesday, June 3, she did not arrive for her first day at her new dairy job. That was when her absence turned into a missing person report. Nearly 50 years on, the case remains open without a body, without belongings, and without a definitive account of what happened between Hamilton and Hastings.

Blades was born in 1957 in Hastings, daughter of Peter Blades and Wagamina Blades, with siblings Lillian and Tony. As a teenager she moved to Hamilton and lived with her sister Lillian, brother-in-law Tom, and their baby daughter Angela. She worked as a shop assistant and had secured a new position to begin on Tuesday after the long weekend.

She did not own a car. Her sister and brother-in-law could not make the 190-miles (about 308 kilometer) drive to Hastings. Hitchhiking was her solution, and it was not unusual in 1975 either. Long-distance public transport across the central North Island was sparse. Intercity buses connected towns on limited schedules; rail options were minimal. Car ownership was high and the roads were full of private traffic. For those without a vehicle, thumbing a ride was commonplace.

Tom dropped her on Cambridge Road, near State Highway 1 (SH1), the longest and most significant road in New Zealand, early that Saturday morning. She dressed for a winter day — a black duffle coat over a green rugby jersey with a white collar and a thorn jersey beneath, light green slacks, brown shoes with yellow laces. She carried a hitchhiker's brown bag and an older shoulder bag. The plan, unshared with her family, was straightforward: Hamilton to Hastings, roughly five and a half hours by bus, shorter if the rides went smoothly.

The first leg went as planned. A woman picked her up in Hamilton, drove her south to Taupo, about ninety miles (145 kilometers) along State Highway 1, and dropped her at the information centre. From there, the record becomes a series of sightings and statements that do not fully align.

Around 10:00 a.m., a witness reported seeing a young woman matching Blades's description, wearing a long green parka, at the corner of Lake Terrace and Titiraupenga Street. Shortly after, a woman working at the information centre recalled speaking with a young woman who planned to visit her parents in Hastings. This woman had left a pack by the centre's door when she came inside.

At 10:30 a.m., a man who knew Blades at the Waipahihi fruit shop saw her walk past. He later said he watched her join another female hitchhiker and saw both get into a dark blue or dark green station wagon heading toward State Highway 5 (SH5), the Napier road. Napier is about twelve miles (twenty kilometers) by road from Hastings. Those details would suggest progress toward her destination.

Yet between noon and 1:30 p.m., other witnesses placed a young woman matching Blades's description at the Spa Hotel in Taupo. Two said they saw her drinking with another girl. A third spoke to a woman who identified herself as Blades and said she got into a red Toyota station wagon outside the bottle shop there. That red Toyota was later reported in a convoy with a motorcycle group at a Taupo service station. In the same time frame, a female witness said she saw two people load a rolled piece of carpet into the back of a red Toyota station wagon.

The cluster of statements complicated the timeline. Police later reasoned that some witnesses may have seen different hitchhikers with similar builds and clothing. Even so, the names of streets, the makes and colors of cars, the times on the clock — those elements stuck to the record and narrowed the window in which Blades was last confidently moving toward Hastings.

The most consequential account from that morning pointed to State Highway 5, the road to Napier, and to a small Japanese station wagon. A truck driver said he saw Blades get into an orange Datsun 120Y station wagon around 10:00 a.m., heading in the direction of Napier. That statement, despite conflicts with the later Spa Hotel sightings, became the last official sighting widely accepted by police at the time.

The driver of the Datsun was described as a balding, large, middle-aged man. Witnesses watched the car veer off SH5 and turn onto Matea Road, a rural dirt track in Rangitaiki about thirty-four miles (about fifty-five kilometers) southeast of Taupo. One fencing contractor drove past and saw the driver and a woman matching Blades's description in the car. When he returned along the road a short time later, the Datsun was parked and empty. What happened in the interval between those two passes has never been established.

About six weeks later, the police received an unsigned letter from a young woman who had been hitchhiking on SH5 that same day. She wrote that she had been picked up by a man in an orange Datsun station wagon heading toward Napier. She felt uncomfortable with his behavior, asked to be let out, and he complied. An elderly couple picked her up soon after, and as they continued, they passed the same Datsun parked by the road. She caught part of the number plate: it began with H, ended with the number 4, and the second letter was either K, V, or E. Her parents told her not to get involved, so she sent the account anonymously. Police appealed publicly for the writer to come forward and provide more, but she did not.

Since the trip was a surprise, no one was waiting for Blades at a specific time. Her absence became clear on Monday when she had not returned to Hamilton, and again on Tuesday when she did not arrive for work. By then, two days had passed, and any immediate trace on roadside verges, in ditches or lay-bys, or along Matea Road was harder to read.

Police from Taupo, Rotorua, Hamilton, and Auckland searched more than 120 miles (about 200 kilometers) of roadway between Tokoroa and Napier. They canvassed the information centre and the Spa Hotel and re-interviewed drivers who might have been on SH1 and SH5 that morning. The size of the search force mirrored the size of the uncertainty.

One detail hampered the investigation from the outset. The initial missing-person notices carried a photograph of Blades with long hair, taken when she had been a bridesmaid. By late May 1975, her hair was in a shorter mullet style. The mismatch may have led some people to dismiss a memory of a short-haired hitchhiker as someone else. A witness said he had thought the hitchhiker he saw was a man because of the haircut. Decades later, in 2018, police released a computer-generated image depicting how she looked at the time with the shorter style. The correction came long after the days when a revised image might have freshened recollections.

The truck driver who reported the orange Datsun later changed aspects of his story on re-interview, and investigators noted the possibility that media coverage had altered his memory. That caution did not displace the central place his account has held in the narrative, but it framed it as a piece of evidence with limits.

Given the emphasis on the orange Datsun, the inquiry widened to everyone who owned, rented, or drove a 120Y station wagon matching the description. Over the six month open inquiry, police examined more than 500 such drivers. Among them were men whose names recur in discussions of the case.

One was John Freeman, who rented an orange Datsun over the long weekend when Blades disappeared. Two weeks later, after police went public about seeking a Datsun, Freeman shot and killed a student at St Cuthbert's College in Epsom, Auckland, and then killed himself. Apart from the rental, investigators found no evidence linking him to Blades's disappearance.

Another was Charlie Hughes, originally from Hamilton, who moved to Sydney and worked as a caretaker. In 1975 he drove an orange Datsun as a company vehicle while employed by a house-removal firm. Accounts at the time said he could not fully explain his movements over the long weekend, and odometer readings showed a distance consistent with a Hamilton–Napier–Hamilton trip. Hughes has repeatedly denied involvement, speaking to newspapers and television over the years to say he had nothing to do with Blades's disappearance. Police interviewed him multiple times in the 1970s and 1980s, again in 1997, and again in 2005. That year, Rotorua detectives flew to Sydney, questioned him for five hours, and collected a voluntary DNA sample. A broadcast on TVNZ's (Television New Zealand Limited) Sunday program suggested that Hughes had been the driver of a Datsun that picked up Blades. Those allegations did not ripen into charges.

A third suspect, unnamed publicly, owned an orange Datsun at the time and drew attention for that reason alone. A fourth was Mervyn Derrick Hinton, a former traffic officer. When asked about the case, he told police, "If you think it was me, prove it." In January 2012, officers drilled through the concrete laundry floor at Hinton's former home in Kawerau (Bay of Plenty), to a depth of about thirty inches (eighty centimeters), then probed another thirty inches (eighty centimeters) beneath. They found nothing. Hinton's daughter, Pauline Barrett, said she was not surprised; she maintained that her father had not owned an orange Datsun station wagon, but an orange Toyota Corolla, and that photographs proved the laundry floor concrete was poured before Blades disappeared. A former police sergeant, Tony Muller, who had been Hinton's friend, insisted that Hinton did own an orange Datsun in 1975 and had ordered both his cars repainted soon after Blades vanished. A 1978 photo from Barrett showed the Toyota still orange at that time. Hinton also did not resemble the balding, heavyset driver described near the Datsun; he had a full head of hair until his death. Muller alleged domestic abuse in Hinton's household; Barrett denied it. Hinton died in 2008. Muller has continued to point to him and speculated that Blades's remains might be under another section of the same house. None of those claims have produced evidence.

The emphasis on vehicle color and brand focused the search, but it also risked narrowing it too far. An orange station wagon on major routes during a long weekend was not rare enough to exclude other possibilities. The letter with the partial plate provided a thread that could not be pulled to its end.

In 2004, the case was reinvestigated. That same year, workers in Huntly, in the Waikato district, found a shallow grave under a garage floor bearing the name "Blades." The inscription raised immediate, painful speculation. Within days it became clear that the name had been set in concrete years earlier as a grim joke. The former property owner apologized to the family. The reinvestigation continued without a discovery.

The losses inside the family deepened the absence. Peter Blades died in 2004. The following year, Mona's brother Tony spoke publicly for the first time, telling the Daily Post that their mother thought about Mona every day, often crying, with no burial and no facts to let grief find its shape. In January 2011, Mona's mother died. The police review that had been reopened in 2004 wound down in 2006.

In 2018, the TVNZ program *Cold Case* reconsidered the investigation. Detectives on the broadcast argued that the original case had fixated too tightly on the orange Datsun. They highlighted the independent sighting of a red Toyota station wagon moving with a motorcycle convoy and suggested that this track had not been sufficiently explored at the time. The episode also floated the idea that Blades had affiliations in gang circles in Auckland and Hamilton and that gang members might have been traveling south toward a gathering in Wellington that weekend, moving through Taupo.

After the broadcast, police clarified their position. Detective Inspector Mark Loper said that the inquiry did not include associates of motorcycle groups. The official view did not adopt the gang theory. Even so, the program's retracing of the red Toyota sighting fit the original witness accounts from outside the Spa Hotel and the service station, which had placed a similar vehicle in company with bikers.

Public tips do not align themselves to official hypotheses. After the episode aired, a man told the Rotorua Daily Post that he had overheard members of Highway 61 — the outlaw motorcycle club founded in New Zealand in 1968 — talk about killing Blades. He said the conversation took place in an apartment in the Grey Lynn, Westmere area of Auckland in the 1970s. The friend he named as the speaker died in 2013. The witness said he had not come forward earlier because he believed from coverage that the orange Datsun driver was responsible, and the friend he heard did not drive an orange Datsun. Highway 61 has chapters in Taupo and Hastings and expanded to Brisbane in the 1980s. Over decades it has been linked to drug dealing, sexual violence, theft, and homicide. None of those general facts fill the gap in this specific case. The man's account added a rumor to a file already heavy with them.

The *Cold Case* broadcast had an enduring practical effect. It re-emphasized that the last hours in Taupo are the critical terrain. It questioned the assumption that Blades had left town that morning, a point the police now state directly. They believe she did not leave Taupo on the day she disappeared. That belief rests on how the sightings intersect and on the limits of the Datsun narrative. It does not, by itself, answer the two questions that structure every missing-person case: where is she, and who is responsible.

If you travel the same roads today, the distances haven't changed. Hamilton to Taupo remains a stretch along State Highway 1. Taupo to Napier remains State Highway 5, bending through forest and pasture. Matea Road remains a side turn into rural quiet. The lines between those places took an eighteen-year-old toward a home she did not reach. What happened along those lines has not been found in the ground or confirmed on paper. The case is still open. The questions are the same ones police asked in June 1975, although most of the people who asked them have long since retired. Somewhere there is an answer about the orange Datsun, about the red Toyota, about the woman who wrote a letter and folded her name away. Somewhere there is a place where the missing day ends.

3

BLOOD SIGNED "CONTRACT"

The story began in the middle of Indiana in the 1980s and ended, for one victim, in a field in DeKalb County in 1991. People had spent a decade arguing about Satanic cults and whether they existed as the public imagined them. In Franklin and Greenwood and at county fairs across Indiana and Ohio, a set of young men tried to make that image real. They chose the symbols that frightened people the most, said the words they believed would give them power, and carried violence with them as they moved from lot to lot. The names that matter are simple. Mark Goodwin. Keith Lawrence. David Lawrence. Jimmy Lee Pinnick. William Anthony Ault and Andrew Wright.

Mark Goodwin's interest in Satanism began when he was a student at Custer Baker Middle School in Franklin. He was about twelve when he started looking up the symbols he saw on album art — the inverted cross, the pentagram — and then moved from images to texts. He read widely, including Anton LaVey's *Satanic Bible*, and took the language at face value. By his mid-teens he had adopted Satanism as a personal identity and wanted others to share it. His family pushed back, especially his father who condemned the ideas outright. Some relatives tried to ignore the subject and wait for it to pass, some cut off contact but none of these stopped him. He collected friends and older acquaintances into a loose circle and then pressed it into a group with a name.

They called themselves Satan's Disciples. The membership was uneven: more males than females, ages ranging from pre-adult to mid-thirties, and a hierarchy that placed Goodwin at the center. He took the title of priest. The settings were barns on the rural edges of Franklin, Indiana, wooded patches that were easy to reach and hard to see into, and an old cemetery near Martinsville. The rituals followed a pattern. The men wore black ceremonial robes; the girls and women were required to wear black lingerie or nothing. The group drank heavily. Goodwin stayed sober and led the rite. He drew a pentagram on the ground, led an invocation to Satan, and said the chant would conjure demons to serve the group's will. Then they killed a cat and drained the blood into a chalice to drink it. The ritual ended in sex without rules.

The details are important for what happened later: the set piece of candles and chant; the idea that the right words could summon help; the idea that blood gave access to something beyond ordinary life; the requirement that the leader stand outside the fog of alcohol while others went along. They carried those assumptions forward. What Goodwin says he would not carry forward was talk of killing a baby as a "true" sacrifice. When some members raised that idea, he left. He was eighteen. He no longer had a group, and he had broken his relationships at home arguing about the person he wanted to be. He decided to reverse that decision on the surface. He told his family he was done with Satanism, moved back in, and hid his beliefs to keep a bed. For two years there were no rituals and no cult. The change was strategic, not ideological.

The next turn came through work. In 1991 Goodwin, then about twenty, took a job at a fast-food restaurant in Greenwood. Two brothers worked there as well, David and Keith Lawrence. Keith was the younger brother, about eighteen or nineteen. David was early twenties. The roles in the family were inverted. Keith led; David followed. Keith had been drawn into Satanism years earlier and had made it a framework for how to think and speak. He collected literature and treated the ideas as a philosophy. He once chased David through their house with a kitchen knife in an argument about beliefs. His parents sent him to a private school in Terre Haute for structure and distance. He came home changed in schedule, not in mind. David stayed close to him because, he said later, Keith was the only family member who treated him with respect. They were a unit. And in Greenwood's back room, one detail gave them away to Goodwin. Keith wore a pentagram necklace.

Goodwin asked about the symbol. Keith talked. The phrases and claims, which the brothers had been using for years, met a listener who wanted to hear them. Goodwin stepped back into the shape he had left. He and Keith wrote out a contract with Satan: twenty years of power in exchange for the soul, signed in blood. David was present but did not sign. The two who had agreed to the terms started going to cemeteries to hold séances, trying to speak with the dead. The efforts did not produce anything they could point to, but the routine mattered more than the result. It renewed a rhythm, it gave a role back to Goodwin and gave Keith a peer who treated his language seriously.

The families reacted the way they had before and the arguments started again. By May 1991 each young man was close to being put out. They chose mobility over another round of fights and signed on with a carnival operator. The choice solved several problems at once. They had jobs and beds, a reason to leave home without a fresh argument, and nights in towns where no one knew them. The routes ran through Indiana and into Ohio. In that circuit, they met a worker from Shelbyville named Jimmy Lee Pinnick.

Pinnick was older than the others at twenty-four. He came from an abusive home, had been in and out of trouble for years, and did not avoid violence. He introduced himself as a Satanist and was admitted into the group. At this point, the circle that moved with the show had a fourth presence near it who wanted in: a twenty-one-year-old worker named William Anthony Ault. He was interested in Satanism, eager for company, and kept at the edges because the three did not want him in the center.

Pinnick's presence changed the balance. He had a criminal history and a willingness to use it. The first death tied to the group came at the end of August. On August 30, 1991, a carnival worker named Andrew Wright, eighteen, from West Milton, Ohio, was found in a field near the Ohio Turnpike, stabbed and left. In the group's account to police, the motive was simple: Wright had been talking about Pinnick's past crimes, and Pinnick wanted him quiet. Pinnick and Keith lured him out, cut his throat, stabbed him, and left him there. No one arrested them then. The only people who knew were the killers, Goodwin and David, and Ault, who learned enough to use the knowledge as leverage. He wanted into the inner circle, and the information looked like a key.

A month later they told him he could join. There would be an initiation. The plan required a location, and a friend of the group named Brenda Ferguson found one: a secluded farm building near Auburn in DeKalb County. On September 25, 1991, after the DeKalb County Free Fair shut down for the night, she dropped the five men at the site. The ritual began with instructions to Ault to lie on a door that had been set up like an altar. They bound and gagged him. Keith read an invocation. Pinnick took a knife that belonged to Keith and made a long cut from the base of Ault's neck down through his abdomen. Keith, David, and Goodwin added their own cuts until an inverted cross was carved into Ault's chest and stomach. Goodwin attempted to cut out Ault's heart. Ault was still alive while all this was happening. Pinnick leaned in and asked whether he was ready to die. Ault whispered something no one has recovered. Pinnick cut his throat and ended it.

After the death, they moved the door into the field with Ault's body on it. They removed the head and hands and tried to burn them. Pinnick later said the head was meant for a friend of Keith's who wanted a skull. Whatever the intent, they left all of the remains at the site. Ferguson returned to pick them up. The group used the cash taken from Ault's pocket to buy food at Arby's and went back to work.

When the fair season ended, the circle broke along job lines. Pinnick returned to Shelbyville. The Lawrence brothers went to the Bahamas with a unit looking for winter work. Goodwin went to Florida and found a job in Hollywood.

Distance changed Goodwin's calculation. He no longer had the nightly presence of the group around him. Without the immediate pressure that comes from shared acts and shared language, he called home. On December 12, 1991, he told his father he had witnessed a torture killing in DeKalb County. His father went to the police. On December 13, officers found Ault's remains in the field, including the skull and hand fragments. On December 30, they arrested Goodwin at his home in Indianapolis and charged him with conspiracy to commit murder. That same day they arrested Pinnick in Shelbyville and charged him with murder. Pinnick confessed. He said he had made the first cut and the last, and he named the others. Goodwin at first said he had only witnessed the killing and would not go further. The names led to warrants for the Lawrence brothers. On January 10, 1992, Keith and David flew into Miami. Customs officers met them at the gate and took them into custody. They were returned to Indiana.

The motive the police settled on for Ault's death followed the earlier pattern. After Wright's killing, Ault knew enough to be a risk The initiation was a pretext for a silence they wanted to enforce. The men pleaded to a range of charges. Pinnick pleaded guilty to murder in Indiana and received sixty years. In Ohio, he pleaded guilty to the murder of Andrew Wright and received twenty-years-to-life. Keith pleaded guilty to conspiracy to commit murder and was sentenced to an indeterminate term of eight to thirty years, followed by twenty years of probation. David pleaded guilty to assisting a criminal and received eighty years. Goodwin pleaded guilty to assisting a criminal and to battery by means of a deadly weapon and received eighty years on each count, to be served concurrently.

In court, Goodwin addressed Ault's mother. He said he was ashamed. He said he did not really know her son but believed he was "good-hearted." She answered him. She said he should be ashamed. She asked what chance her son had now and told him she would not feel sorry for him. The exchange was brief and shaped by a fact that cannot be changed by words. Ault had been led into a building by people he wanted to call friends.

The years after the sentencing add coda rather than closure. Pinnick tried to appeal in 1995 and failed. Goodwin converted to Christianity in prison and told a reporter that Satanism was dangerous. He used Ault as an example of a person who "didn't make it," a formulation that puts the decision in the wrong place but the truth still stands: Ault did not make it because the group decided he would not. Keith's prison record included two college degrees and no major disciplinary problems. He was released in 2006 to begin his twenty-year probation. The county where he lived with his parents did not have an in-home detention program, so the conditions were eased to regular probation. In November that year, he pleaded guilty to public intoxication and received 180 days in jail. Two felony counts — criminal confinement and battery — were filed and then dismissed.

The final image worth holding is not the robes or the chant or the inverted cross cut into skin. It is the simple fact of movement. The group moved because the carnival moved. They used that to their advantage. They killed, ate a meal purchased with the victim's money, and went back to their posts. The people who welcomed families to the midway in the morning had spent part of the night in a field with a door and a knife and a body. The distance between those two facts is not large. It is a short drive and an early shift.

4

WEDNESDAY CALLS

Dorothy Jane Scott disappeared on May 28, 1980 after months of alarming phone calls from a man she did not know. Four years later, a construction worker uncovered her remains at Santa Ana Canyon Road. The calls, the disappearance from a hospital parking lot, the burned car, and the fragmentary recovery of her remains are the fixed points of a case that remains unsolved decades later. The record that survives is sparse and methodical: names, dates, distances, objects left behind. The gaps, including who placed the calls and who drove her car away from the hospital that night, have never been closed.

Dorothy was born on April 23, 1948, in Anaheim, California. In 1976 she gave birth to her son, Sean. She was a single mother; Sean's father, Dennis Terry, lived far away in Missouri and was not involved in day-to-day care. By 1980, Dorothy was thirty-two, Sean was four, and they lived with Dorothy's aunt, Shanti Scott, in Stanton, about twenty minutes from Anaheim, where Jacob and Vera still resided, her father and mother. Dorothy handled back-office duties for two adjoining businesses at 517 South Brookhurst Street — Swinger's Psych Shop and Custom John's Head Shop — co-owned in part by her father. The shops fit their era: rock music and posters, back-lit rooms, drug paraphernalia next door, the lingering color of 1960s and 1970s counterculture. Dorothy's role sat behind the scenes, keeping the operation organized.

Descriptions of her personality are consistent. Co-workers called her dependable and organized. Friends and family called her a devoted mother. She was a regular churchgoer, a quiet introvert. She did not drink, did not use drugs, did not date. Her routine centered on work and her child. Each day she dropped Sean at her parents' house, worked long hours, and returned to him at night.

In the first months of 1980, the routine was disrupted by anonymous calls to her home and workplace. The caller was a man. His voice was familiar enough that Dorothy told her mother and others she thought she knew it but was not able to name him. The content swung between declaration and threat. He said he loved her but also that he would kill her. He described how he would get her alone and dismember her so she could not be found. He said he was watching, then proved it by recounting what she had worn or done that day. On one occasion he told her to look outside; she found a dead rose on the windshield of her 1973 station wagon. The calls continued for months. One of the last calls unnerved her enough that she began karate lessons. She discussed buying a firearm with her mother and co-workers but before she can, she was abducted.

The day of her disappearance began with normal errands. On May 28, 1980, Dorothy dropped Sean at her parents' house and went to an employee meeting. During the meeting, co-worker Conrad Bostron appeared ill. He was sweating, unable to sit still, with an inflamed red rash on his arm. Seeing this, Dorothy insisted on taking him to the hospital and another co-worker, Pam Head, joined them. Dorothy drove her Toyota station wagon. First, they stopped at her parents' home so she could update them on the situation and check on Sean. She changed her scarf from a gray or black one to a red one, then continued on to University of California, Irvine Medical Center (UCI Medical Center).

The diagnosis justified the urgency. A black widow spider bite explained Conrad's symptoms and required monitoring. They remained at the hospital through the day and into the night, waiting. Dorothy and Pam stayed together in the lobby, reading and talking, leaving only for brief bathroom breaks. Around 11:00 p.m., Conrad was discharged. He was still unsteady, so Dorothy offered to bring the car around to the front entrance. Conrad and Pam went to the pharmacy to pick up his prescription. They expected to meet Dorothy at the curb within minutes.

When they reached the hospital entrance, Dorothy was not there. After roughly fifteen to twenty minutes of waiting, Pam and Conrad walked toward the lot where Dorothy had originally parked. Before they arrived, a car came fast toward them with its high beams on. The lights were bright enough to blind their eyes. The station wagon swerved, narrowly missing them, then turned out of the lot, switched off its headlights, turned right from the hospital, and disappeared. The two were left at the curb with no explanation. They considered that Dorothy might have had an emergency involving her son and needed to go home quickly before returning. They waited two hours but she did not come back. They called Jacob and Vera; the couple had not heard from their daughter. Pam decided to call the UCI police. The initial response reflected a standard posture toward missing adults: Dorothy was free to do whatever she wanted. However, the posture changed several hours later.

Between 4:30 and 5:00 a.m., authorities found Dorothy's station wagon in Santa Ana, about nine miles (fifteen kilometers) from the hospital, engulfed in flames in an alleyway. Dorothy was not inside the vehicle. Searches in the following days found no sign of her. The fire moved the case from uncertainty to suspicion, but there was still little to hold onto beyond a timeline and a burned car in a separate city.

The question of how the car got there acquired layers. There were mentions about another car leaving ahead of Dorothy's, turning the same way out of the hospital. Those mentions were not uniform. If true, the detail could suggest more than one person involved, one driving Dorothy's car and another leading or following, and a second vehicle available later to leave the scene where the Toyota was set on fire. If false, the possibilities narrow to a single driver who either disposed of the body first and then burned the car or set the fire and left on foot or via a waiting ride. No witnesses came forward to say they saw the car set alight, a person walking away, or suspicious activity in the alley. The interval between the hospital and the fire — four to five hours — left room for multiple scenarios and no firm answer.

The calls did not end with the disappearance. About a week later, Vera answered the house phone. The male caller asked whether she was related to Dorothy Scott. When she said yes, he said, "I've got her," and hung up. Police asked the family not to publicize the calls or the disappearance, to reduce false leads. After a week with no progress, Jacob spoke to the Santa Ana Register. The paper published a story and offered a $2,500 reward for information. On the day of publication, the paper's editor, Pat Riley, received a call from an anonymous male. The caller said, "I killed her. I killed Dorothy Scott. She was my love. I caught her cheating with another man. She denied having someone else. I killed her." He authenticated himself by referencing details that had not been released: that Dorothy had changed from a dark scarf to a red one, and that Conrad had suffered a spider bite and that Dorothy had taken him to UCI Medical Center. He also said Dorothy had called him from the hospital hours before her disappearance.

The claim that Dorothy phoned him did not align neatly with what Pam reported. She had been with Dorothy in the lobby all day and night except for brief bathroom breaks and said Dorothy had not made any calls. The point remains a gap. It is possible to imagine a call made in a restroom or during one of the short intervals when they were apart, but there are no phone records that settled the question either way.

Investigators contacted Dennis, Sean's father. Distance made him an unlikely suspect; he was over 3,500 miles (over 5,600 km) away in Missouri. Co-workers from the psych and head shops were questioned repeatedly and ruled out. Because Dorothy worked in the back office, it seemed unlikely a customer had fixated on her, though the possibility cannot be completely excluded on that basis alone. Sex offenders in the area were checked without result. Those in Dorothy's social circle described a woman without enemies and without an obvious person who disliked her enough to harm her.

Dorothy's parents and detectives turned to psychics. The case had little physical evidence and few leads. Months turned into years. The anonymous male continued to call Vera almost every Wednesday afternoon. He used short phrases — "I've got her," "I killed her," "Where is Dorothy?" — a narrow set of statements that served only to remind the family of what they did not know. Police installed a recorder at the Scott residence. The voice was gruff and obviously disguised. No one recognized it. Efforts to trace the calls failed; he never stayed on the line long enough. The timing suggested he knew the family's routine and called when he expected Vera to be home. In April 1984, Jacob answered. The caller hung up. The calls stopped for a long period.

The break in the case came not from the phone or a confession but from a construction site. On August 6, 1984, a worker at Santa Ana Canyon Road uncovered the remains of a dog. Beneath that burial was a set of human remains: pelvis, arm, two thighs, and a skull. With the remains were a turquoise ring and a watch that had stopped at 12:30 a.m. on May 29, 1980, the night Dorothy disappeared. Vera recognized the ring as Dorothy's. Dental records confirmed the identification. An autopsy could not determine a cause of death due to decomposition and the partial nature of what was recovered. Shortly after the public announcement of the discovery, Jacob and Vera received one more call. The male voice asked, "Is Dorothy there?" There were no further answers in the years that followed.

The case remains cold. Jacob died in 1994. Vera died in 2002. There has been no official suspect named, and no arrest.

To this day, theories are still circulating. The first suspect is a man called Mike Butler. He was described as deeply religious, with alternative beliefs and possible involvement in cult-like activity. A frame that some see as consistent with the burial detail of a dog above Dorothy's remains, though the significance of that element is not established. He was an "army brat"; his mother was a New Zealand war bride, his father an Army captain. The family settled in Southern California after his father retired. He went to Fullerton Union High School and later California State University, majoring in English. He was athletic, voted MVP (Most Valuable Player) in cross-country. Drafted into the U.S. Army at age twenty, he served in Hohenfels, Germany, in 1967 after basic training. In Germany he wrote for Stars and Stripes News, an independent news organization that provides news and information to U.S. military communities around the world, and served as a public information and media officer, and photographer. After his service, he became a roadie for rock bands, including work with the Beach Boys and for his sister's band. His sister, an accomplished musician and singer, worked for a time at the Swinger's shop in Anaheim alongside Dorothy. Mike settled in Orange County and worked maintenance at a machine shop across the street from the shops where Dorothy and his sister worked. The proximity could explain a voice that sounded familiar to Dorothy without a clear name attached. It could also have given someone the opportunity to watch her routine. Mike Butler died on June 28, 2014 from health complications. If he was involved, his death would remove the possibility of any confession. The theory rests on proximity, a possible path to a familiar voice, and his background, which might align with elements around the burial.

A second theory compares the case to the Golden State Killer, also known as the East Area Rapist and linked to the Visalia Ransacker cases. The points of contact are the phone calls — pre-crime and, in at least one instance, a call a decade later — the stalking, and a focus on women in vulnerable domestic contexts. He moved to Southern California in 1979. Dorothy's case reads as personal in a way the Golden State Killer's pattern does not. The caller said he loved her and referred to a cheating accusation. Dorothy was taken from a hospital setting rather than attacked at home, which was the offender's usual pattern. The comparison highlights superficial similarities, but there are some clear divergences too.

The third theory is the most straightforward: a secret boyfriend or former boyfriend. This would fit the caller's claim of love, the "cheating" accusation, and the knowledge of Dorothy's day-to-day life. It would also explain a phone number and the ability to reach her parents' residence. The counter-points are also simple. People close to Dorothy said she did not date, worked long hours, and spent her evenings with Sean. She lived with her aunt. If she had been absent at night or asked her parents to take Sean more than usual, someone might have noticed. All that is known is what has been reported by the people around her; it cannot exclude a relationship that others did not see.

Across all the theories, the same fixed events define what can be said with certainty. Dorothy was harassed by a caller for months in early 1980. She took up self-defense classes and discussed buying a firearm. On May 28, 1980 she drove Conrad and Pam to UCI Medical Center, checked on her son in between, changed to a red scarf, and remained with Pam through the evening. At about 11:00 p.m. she left the lobby to retrieve her car. Within minutes her station wagon nearly struck her two co-workers under high beams, swerved, and drove off with the lights off, turning right out of the hospital. Hours later the car burned in Santa Ana. Calls to Vera and to the newspaper followed, including details that had not been public. For years, the same man phoned on Wednesdays and hung up when Jacob answered. In August 1984, Dorothy's remains were found beneath a dog burial at Santa Ana Canyon Road, with her turquoise ring and a watch stopped at 12:30 a.m. on May 29. The cause of death could not be determined.

The story does not end. It merely rests. The remains were identified. The parents died without resolution. Sean grew up with the public outline of events that surrounded his mother's disappearance. The person who called Vera on Wednesdays had a script that never varied much. Each sentence kept the family suspended in the moment after May 28, 1980. There is no closing legal paragraph to place here. There is only the record of what happened and the unanswered question of who dialed the phone and who drove away from the hospital entrance with the high beams pointed at two people waiting on the curb.

5

THE BUSANG MIRAGE

On December 13, 1993, a prospector in the jungles of Borneo said he had found what every mining investor hopes to hear: a strike big enough to change the map. The hills were volcanic, the theory familiar — gold often sits in and around ancient volcanic systems — and the core that went to the lab came back with grades that made sense to people who wanted to believe. The property was called Busang. The company tied to it was a small Canadian junior that traded like a thousand others until this set of results lifted it out of obscurity.

The person on the ground was Michael de Guzman, a Filipino geologist who had spent years in Indonesia without breaking into the upper tiers of major firms. The promoter who would carry the story to North American investors was David Walsh, a Western Canadian stock man who needed a property and a narrative. Between them stood John Felderhof, a risk-tolerant geologist of good reputation who had been associated with a real Indonesian mine. The roles were clear in practice: de Guzman controlled the site, the samples, and the day-to-day; Felderhof provided technical credibility; Walsh told the market what the labs seemed to be saying.

Junior mining shares are built on assays. Rock comes out of the ground, is split, crushed, and sent to a lab; a number comes back; analysts publish;

the stock moves. At Busang, the early numbers were strong. The company's market value climbed from the low single digits to levels juniors rarely reach. Each round of results appeared to extend the zone. Commentary from Bay Street and Wall Street amplified the effect: dispatches from Indonesia, comparisons to "elephant deposits," charts that made the hills and drill collars feel immediate. Money arrived. De Guzman cleared jungle, opened pads, and expanded drilling with better equipment. The more holes they reported, the more the equity rose. The logic was circular and, in that phase, effective.

Behind the numbers was a mechanism. De Guzman, knowing there was no gold in the rock, salted the samples. The method was simple and careful. Core pulled from the ground was supposed to be split in half, with one half archived on site for verification and the other half crushed and sent to labs. He brought crushed core into a locked shed and added fine gold to the pulp — initially from his wedding ring, later from small purchases of placer gold panned by locals in nearby rivers. He calculated how much to add to produce grades that looked plausible rather than spectacular, the kind of numbers that inspire confidence rather than suspicion. If a salted sample shows too much metal, geologists balk. If it looks right, the story holds.

Where an auditor expected to see half the core stored in tidy racks, de Guzman offered less than a tenth retained, with an explanation. He cited the "nugget effect," the genuine phenomenon in which coarse, unevenly distributed gold can produce erratic numbers from one split to the next, and argued that he needed to crush and assay all the material to get a proper average. To a visiting accountant, that rendered many cross-checks impossible. If half the core is gone, independent labs cannot re-assay against the original; if the only remaining material has been milled to dust, visual checks for coarse gold are meaningless. To address another potential tell, de Guzman's river-gold source was made to fit the story with a volcanic-pool theory: if the deposit had been remobilized by hydrothermal fluids, flake-like shapes could appear. The auditors accepted the framework. The company's website announced success. The stock lifted again.

As Busang 1 filled in, maps were redrawn to suggest scale. If gold was in a structure, perhaps it extended into the next. The company moved to "Busang 2," and when the drills there brought more strong lab numbers, Walsh sought listings beyond the junior Alberta exchange. NASDAQ and the Toronto Stock Exchange followed. Each regulatory milestone was framed as external validation: if the company could list there, then the company had cleared serious hurdles, and the core must be as good as reported. The stock approached $300 a share. The company's paper value touched roughly $6 billion. On paper, men who had struggled in their trades for years were rich. They sold some shares — enough to transform their circumstances, not so much as to abandon the narrative — and the market read that as insurance rather than a signal.

The Indonesian state, which had never been gentle with natural-resource concessions, made its own move. In August 1996, officials revoked Bre-X's exploration permit and opened the property to other firms. A fight among majors began, with Jakarta poised to pick its preferred partners and to keep a large share for the government. For a hoax that depended on a controlled worksite, this was the beginning of the end. Other geologists would drill their own holes within a few feet of de Guzman's collars. They would keep the chain of custody tight from rig to lab. They would cut, crush, and assay without letting local hands touch the pulp between steps.

Before that scrutiny arrived in full, there was an "accidental" fire. De Guzman's site records burned. In the narrative that followed, the loss of maps, logs, and residual samples helped obscure what had been done. The government imposed a new partnership. Freeport-McMoRan, an experienced operator in the region, took a controlling technical role. Bre-X's stake was cut to forty-five percent and the market punished the dilution. The company responded with a new, larger reserve estimate to offset the value erosion. Where analysts had been told to expect fifty plus million ounces, they were now told to expect 70 million. The stock, briefly rocked, found its footing. The shareholder meeting in Toronto in early 1997 had the look of a victory lap: the chief geologist delivering a slide deck, a promoter who could say he had kept the deal alive under pressure, and a room full of people whose brokerage statements supported the applause.

In Indonesia, Freeport's drills were spinning a few yards from the collars that had supposedly tapped the richest ore. Their samples contained no gold. The phone call that followed was direct: get back here and explain. Three years of releases, billions of dollars of paper value, and a series of almost cinematic milestones were about to meet a number that mattered, and that number was 0.

On the morning of the flight back to the site, de Guzman boarded a helicopter. It climbed over the rainforest. When the pilot looked into the rear, the seat was empty. De Guzman had gone out the door at 400 to 500 feet (about 120 to 160 meters). Three days later, the army announced that it had found his body, badly decomposed and partly scavenged by animals. The pilot had logged a GPS position; the delay made little sense to those who knew what that meant. The remains were not shown to his family. Then came the rumors: that he had been pushed, that he had staged the fall and vanished, that he was alive under another name. The official statement was suicide.

Freeport's twin holes kept returning nothing. Independent check drilling — tight security, strict custody — found no gold where Bre-X had claimed "pools" of it. The market's turn was swift. The "largest gold deposit in the world" could not survive side-by-side holes that showed barren rock. The stock that had been a vehicle for hope became, quickly, a zero. Investors who had put retirement money into a Canadian junior lost savings overnight.

In the aftermath, the principals scattered along predictable lines. Walsh, who had denied knowing about any fraud, moved to the Bahamas and died of a heart attack two years later. Felderhof maintained a comfortable life in the Cayman Islands, with the benefits of a jurisdiction that did not extradite Canadian white-collar defendants at the time. No one served a day in jail for the central act: selling salted assays as real. Bringing criminal charges would have meant proving intent — what executives knew and when. Each could claim, credibly to some, that they only relayed what the labs reported and that any wrongdoing lay with trusted subordinates. The one man who could have tied it all together — if he'd wanted — fell from a helicopter into the jungle.

The Bre-X collapse did change the plumbing of the market. Canadian regulators tightened technical disclosure standards in mining. The idea was to make it harder to repeat a con that depended on lax custody of core, thin archives, and third-party reports written off site with no direct verification. The appetite for a "company-making" deposit has never left the junior sector; neither has the dynamic in which a stock's rise is taken as proof that underlying facts must be sound. In Busang's case, the rise masked the absence of ore.

6

GLORIAVALE CHRISTIAN COMMUNITY

New Zealand's South Island is a landscape of almost unimaginable beauty, a place of glistening lakes and snow-capped mountains. Its scenery is so idyllic that it seems impossible for anything sinister to take root there. Yet, nestled in a valley on the island's remote west coast, a reclusive community lives entirely cut off from the modern world. This community is known as Gloriavale. What began decades ago as a small, enthusiastic group of devout Christians has, over the years, mutated into a secretive and disturbing cult, built around a twisted predator.

The Gloriavale Christian Community is currently home to about 600 men, women, and children. They live, work, and pray together, almost completely severed from outside society. Documentaries have offered a surface-level glimpse into their lives, showing children playing and families eating together. But even in these sanitized portrayals, the red flags are impossible to miss. The community practices arranged marriages. Everyone, including small children, is required to wear a uniform. Multiple families are forced to live together in cramped hostels. And at the center of it all is the leader, a man who wields ultimate authority over every life. The devotion he commands is absolute, with members stating they would lay down their lives for him.

This facade of pious harmony conceals a reality steeped in controversy and abuse. The people of Gloriavale are forced to live a lie, brainwashed into believing their twisted existence is the only path to heaven. From birth, they are taught that they are the chosen people and that if they ever leave, their souls are automatically damned to hell. It is a utopia custom-built for its founder, where people are treated like slaves, abuse is encouraged, and merely having an independent opinion risks severe punishment or exile. This is not a historical footnote; the group exists to this day, and as recently as July 2025, one of its leaders pleaded guilty to serious crimes.

The architect of this world was Neville Cooper. Born in 1926 in Queensland, Australia, he grew up under a strict father and a mean mother. After clashing with his father, who owned a fruit shop, he was kicked out at sixteen. A brief stint in the Air Force, compounded by his brother's death in the war, reportedly led to a mental health decline. Around age 21, while recovering at an aunt's house, Neville experienced a religious awakening. He claimed God told him his purpose was to preach the gospel as a minister.

He threw himself into the Bible, adopting extreme, hellfire-and-brimstone beliefs: any sin meant damnation, and women must be subservient to men. At his new church, he met Gloria Perry. He was twenty-one; she was fifteen or sixteen. Described as sweet and quiet, she was easy for him to control. They would go on to have sixteen children. At twenty-three, Neville started his own traveling ministry, "The Voice of Deliverance," preaching an energetic, charismatic message of piety or damnation from a large tent. He gained a following and a pilot's license, flying himself on missions. On Christmas Eve 1965, he survived a plane crash with three others, an event the media called a miracle. Neville believed it was a sign he was destined for more.

In 1967, he moved his family to New Zealand. He clashed with local church leaders, finding them insufficiently extreme and attempting to take over their congregations. In 1969, after a final falling out, he formed his own community with members who left to follow him, believing in his special connection to God. They became known as the "Cooperites." By the late 1970s, they settled at Springbank, on New Zealand's South Island, in a commune called the Christian Church at Springbank. From this point, Neville began to exert total control. His vision was a self-sustaining utopia, separated from the world. Followers had to sell all their possessions and give the money to the church.

He established a rigid hierarchy: he was the "Overseeing Shepherd," followed by "Shepherds," "Servants," and the general population, with women at the bottom. The community lived by a literal interpretation of the King James Bible. Individualism was forbidden. Members could not have their own opinions, choose their jobs, or marry who they loved. Neville ruled through fear and shame. The primary fear was eternal damnation. If any family member was deemed sinful, the entire family was publicly shamed, creating an environment where people would inform on their own relatives to stay in Neville's good graces.

Children were taught to fear the "evil" outside world. One former member recalled being told that as a child, she deserved to be "stoned with rocks constantly." They were taught that the more severe the sin, the hotter the flames. Lessons on the property included creationism, such as how dinosaurs fit on Noah's ark by Noah simply taking baby ones. No birthdays or holidays were celebrated.

The community was aggressively male-dominated. Women were taught to be completely subservient, existing only as a "help meet" for their husbands, who were their "head." Women wore a uniform of long skirts, high-necked, long-sleeved tops, and head coverings to show their subjugation. Pants, makeup, and jewelry were forbidden as vanity. Even when swimming, girls wore their dresses. The costume designer for *The Handmaid's Tale's* television adaptation later cited the cult as an inspiration. Neville's rationale was that men could not control themselves, so it was a woman's job not to tempt them. He had a particular fixation on elbows, which were never to be shown.

Life was run on a strict schedule of communal meals and assigned chores. Women would wake as early as 2:00 a.m. for cooking and cleaning, while children were forced into hard labor from as young as 5 years old. Any man who voiced dissent was forced into a "men's meeting," where leaders would berate him, sometimes for days, until he repented or was punished.

Marriages were arranged by Neville to manage "sexual urges." Wives were never allowed to refuse sex; upon marriage, they lost the right to say no. Consent was not a concept in the group. Neville believed girls were "considered a woman" as soon as they had their first period, around age twelve or thirteen, and that they were capable of being mothers then. One former member stated she was considered an adult at age 10. The only reason Neville made them wait until age sixteen was because of New Zealand's laws. These rules were codified in a cult-written book, *What We Believe*. When Neville implemented these rules, some original members left, but most remained, trapping their families in decades of abuse.

Neville was physically abusive to his own children, especially his sons, and likely his wife Gloria as well. He taught his followers to discipline their families the same way. Physical abuse was rampant, with most men beating their wives and children, a practice that was completely normalized. One former member described how being beaten by a violent father became the norm, and how he learned to take it without flinching or crying, turning his endurance into a source of pride. Teachers at the school would also beat children.

Alongside this, sexual abuse was pervasive. Neville sexualized everything, creating a bizarre contrast to the community's puritanical rules. Leaders and other men would openly grope girls serving meals, rubbing their bodies or untying their dresses as they passed, often in front of their own families. The girls, taught to never question a man and that they had no bodily autonomy, felt they had no choice but to let it happen. This behavior by the leaders signaled to other men that it was acceptable. The girls were made to feel it was their fault, as they had been taught men could not control themselves.

Neville's predation was methodical. He encouraged parents to have sex in front of their young children, as young as six or seven, to "educate" them. He held group "marriage counseling" where he would have couples lay out blankets and order them to have sex in front of each other, while he watched. He would invite newlywed couples to dinner, only to force the husband to lie next to Neville's wife, Gloria, and watch as Neville undressed and violated the new bride. He did this to his own son, Phil, and his wife, Sandy, who were terrified to refuse. This abuse caused severe issues within their marriage. This was not Phil's first experience; as a teenager, Phil had confided in Neville about pain in his testicles, and Neville had proceeded to assault his son under the pretense of an examination.

Another ritual involved a spa room on the property. Neville and other shepherds would get into the pool completely naked, put a pornographic movie on a projector, and then force teenage girls to strip down and get into the pool with them. This, he claimed, was part of their education, preparing them for marriage.

The arranged marriage process was a clinical ordeal. A man would request a wife, and the leaders would consult bloodline lists to avoid inbreeding, selecting a suitable girl. After "praying" on it, they would inform the man of God's "choice." Often, the couple did not even know each other. The man would then ask the woman for her hand, and she would go pray about it before returning with her "yes." This was just a formality, as the women had no real choice. After an engagement of about a month, a large wedding ceremony was held. After exchanging vows, the bride, now the man's property, had to sign a document effectively agreeing to be her husband's sex slave, waiving her right to ever refuse anything sexual. In the middle of the reception, the newly married couple would be led to a "honeymoon suite" to consummate the marriage immediately, sometimes with Neville present, before returning to the party.

Over the years, twelve of Neville's sixteen children managed to escape, but those who left were completely cut off from the members who remained. Inside the cult, women were expected to have as many babies as possible, as contraceptives were forbidden under any circumstances. Even if a doctor advised a woman not to have more children for life-threatening medical reasons, Neville would make the woman write a letter to her doctor rejecting the medical advice. When complications arose during childbirth, women were allowed to go to a hospital. But if the baby did not survive, the mother received no emotional support. She was expected to return to work immediately, with no time to grieve or recover. She was also made to believe the death was her fault, a punishment from God.

Former member Theo Pratt described how her mother, after delivering a stillborn son named Samuel at a hospital, was sent back to the commune with his body in a small box. While she was in bed, distraught, the leaders came to her room, not to offer sympathy, but to take Samuel's body. They refused to tell her where they were taking him. Stillborn babies were reportedly buried in a separate, overgrown, and forgotten part of the property. She was forced right back to work, expected to completely turn off her grief.

In the early 1990s, with the group expanding, Neville moved the cult to an even more isolated plot of land on the west coast, about an hour's drive from Greymouth. He had large hostels built, with several families forced to live together in very tight quarters. Just before the move, Neville's wife, Gloria, died of a brain tumor. He named the new commune the "Gloriavale Christian Community" in her honor. Neville himself remarried twice; his second wife, who was in her eighties, died shortly after, but his third wife, Ruth, was only seventeen years old when he was in his sixties. It was around this time that he had everyone change their names; he became "Hopeful Christian," while others adopted names like "Willing Disciple," "Steadfast Joy," and, for one baby girl, "Submissive."

Gloriavale is worth a lot of money. The cult owns several profitable businesses, including a massive dairy farm, an air service for short flights, and a deer processing business, which together bring in millions of dollars per year. The cult members, including children, operate all of these businesses, working upwards of 70 hours a week or more for zero pay. Neville built a community of worshippers who ran his profitable enterprises as slave labor. He claimed they were paid by receiving free rent, food, and healthcare, but if anyone left, they walked away with nothing.

Shortly after the move to Gloriavale, Neville's past caught up with him. A former member named Yvette Olsen, who had escaped the Springbank commune years earlier, courageously went to the police. She reported that in the early 1980s, when she was sixteen, she had developed a "secret friendship" with a fourteen-year-old boy named Tim. They ran away together but were tracked down and dragged back. Neville forced the teenagers to get married in a secret ceremony. For two years, he kept them separated and waged a campaign to destroy Yvette's self-worth, forcing her to call herself degrading names like "Harlot" and constantly beg for forgiveness.

After two years, Neville insisted they needed "marriage counseling" before they could live together, which he himself would conduct. During Yvette's private sessions, he subjected her to a bizarre and brutal assault for three days straight. He forced her to lie on a bed while he assaulted her with a long wooden object soaked in oil. He told her he had measured Tim's genitals to make sure the object was the right size. He threatened that if she tried to get up, he would ensure she and Tim could never be together. Yvette and Tim eventually escaped with their child. She decided to go to the police years later, after her niece confided that she had also been assaulted by a Gloriavale man.

Police raided Gloriavale in 1994, and Neville was arrested. He claimed he had simply given Yvette the object to use on herself as "therapy." Four other victims came forward, and Neville's own son, Phil, testified against his father about the sexual abuse he had endured. Neville was convicted of ten counts of indecent assault and sentenced to six years, but he appealed and was granted a new trial. This time, he was found guilty of only three charges and sentenced to five years, but he was released after serving less than two.

Because the followers were so cut off from the world, they had no idea what Neville was actually convicted of. The leaders fed them lies, pushing the narrative that Neville was being persecuted for spreading God's word. The leaders went to great lengths to maintain this ignorance, even going through old newspapers used to start fires and cutting out any articles they didn't want the followers to see. Neville continued to send orders from prison, and when he was released, he returned to Gloriavale as a hero who had suffered for his faith.

Tragedy continued to strike within the community. In June 2015, a fourteen-year-old girl named Prayer Ready, who had Down syndrome, died in one of the community's "isolation rooms." These rooms were used to quarantine the sick. Prayer was ill and had been sent to the room. Her dinner was delivered, but the food had not been cut into small pieces, which she required as she struggled to chew properly. Her mother, Sharon, was in the room but had her back turned and did not notice until

Prayer began to choke on a piece of meat. Sharon panicked. Another adult in the room tried to help but was unsuccessful. When they tried to get help, they found they were trapped; the door handles had been disabled. Eventually, someone climbed out of a window yelling for help. By the time help arrived, it was too late, and Prayer Ready was dead.

According to former members, it was common practice to disable the door handles, supposedly to prevent healthy children from wandering into the room. Concerns about this dangerous practice had been ignored in the past. An inquest ultimately ruled that the disabled handles played no part in Prayer's death because they had access to a window, a conclusion many disagreed with. The cult's leader, Hopeful Christian (Neville), later approached Prayer's grieving father, Clem. He told Clem that he could take comfort in the fact that now that Prayer was dead, she would not be sexually molested by anyone in the community. This comment deeply shook Clem.

In 2018, another death occurred under strange circumstances when Sincere Standtrue, a twenty-year-old man, was found unresponsive in the cult's paint shop where he worked. It is widely believed he died by suicide. Sincere's sister, Rose, has said he was treated horribly by the community. Sincere was deaf, and Neville would become angry when he couldn't hear orders. Other boys picked up on this and bullied Sincere, mocking him, calling him names, and locking him in bathroom stalls. He was also picked on by teachers. When he took his hearing aids out to stop the mockery, he got in more trouble for not being able to hear. He told his sister his boss had beaten him with a pipe, and there were reports he had been sexually abused as well.

Two months before his death, Sincere had been removed from his family's home and forced to live in the "men's room," a place seen as a disgrace, reserved for single men or those whose wives had escaped. Sincere had repeatedly asked the leaders to be assigned a wife but was always denied because he had not been allowed to sign the community's "commitment." v In a cult where a person's entire value was based on having a family, this denial would have been devastating, making him feel worthless. Rose now believes her brother, who was smart but struggled to verbalize, may have had autism. Instead of being supported, he was ostracized, isolated, and bullied. An inquest into his death, concluded in March 2025, ruled it accidental, likely caused by a "blacking out game" popular in the cult, a ruling his sister disputes.

Prayer Ready's sister, Connie, escaped the cult after her sister's death. In 2018, she went to the police with allegations of child abuse against her father, Clem. She stated he would severely beat all his children, including Prayer, sometimes for no reason. Clem later blamed his actions on the cult's culture, which encouraged violent discipline, and the exhaustion from working seventy-hour weeks. He pleaded guilty, received supervision, and was ordered to pay damages and attend counseling. This conviction was a turning point for Clem. He began to reassess the cult's teachings on violence and its sexual attitudes toward his wife and daughters. When he started asking questions, the leaders kicked him out. He and his wife, Sharon, unable to leave their children, grandchildren, and Prayer's grave, became "uninvited guests," living in an old building on the edge of the property.

The legal troubles mounted. After multiple investigations into forced labor were dismissed with the ruling that the members were "volunteers," former members brought multi-million dollar lawsuits in 2022 and 2023. The church argued the members signed the commitment of their own free will. The women argued they were born into the cult and conditioned since birth, groomed to be cheap labor and to provide unlimited sex. This time, the court agreed with the former members, ruling they were employees, not volunteers, a major victory that exposed decades of forced child labor.

Neville Cooper died of cancer in 2018 at the age of ninety-two. His son Phil remarked that his father would have to answer to God for the lives he destroyed and would likely go to hell. The cult, however, has endured, and the allegations of abuse have continued. In 2022, Joseph Hope was imprisoned for assaulting a girl under twelve, sometimes while his wife and children were in the same room. That same year, Timothy Disciple pleaded guilty to assaulting a twelve-year-old girl and two other young victims. Fervent Ben-Kenan was sentenced for abusing young girls in their beds at night between 2004 and 2018. Jonathan Benjamin was sentenced in 2024 to nearly twelve years in prison for abusing multiple children, one as young as five, between 1986 and 2017. When leaders found out about abuse, the offender was merely made to repent and apologize publicly.

The leaders, of course, were often offenders themselves. Howard Temple, an eighty-five-year-old former U.S. Navy engineer, took over as Overseeing Shepherd after Neville's death. In July 2025, Temple pleaded guilty to multiple charges of indecent assault against women and children. He also admitted that the community had a policy preventing members from reporting crimes to outside authorities. A new leader, forty-eight-year-old Steven Stanfast, has since taken over, claiming he is bringing real change.

Police investigations are reportedly ongoing. As of 2024, police have identified more than 138 victims of physical and sexual abuse and over 400 crimes, with many men charged or under investigation. This is not the full picture, as many are still too scared or brainwashed to come forward. Before his death, Neville had also established sister communes in India. Five girls from Gloriavale were sent to India to marry men in the new sect, populate the commune, and serve as manual labor, a situation that has prompted human trafficking concerns. A leader of the Indian sect, Faithful Stronghold, made a disturbing admission that Indian men are very forceful and that it is part of the culture to force themselves on women.

Despite the decades of abuse, people have been fleeing. The Gloriavale Leavers Support Trust was started in 2019 to help escapees, providing housing, financial aid, and emotional support. Former members, including Rosanna Overcomer and Pearl Valor, have been central to these efforts and the lawsuits. These women, once forced into uniforms and subjugation, are now seen wearing clothes they choose, looking confident and happy. Over the years, at least 300 people have left Gloriavale. But as of 2024, about 600 people remain, more than half of them children, and they are not safe.

7

NANJING UNIVERSITY MURDER

January 19, 1996 carried the kind of cold that tightens the jaw and shortens a person's stride. In Nanjing, a sanitation worker was still out on the pavements when most of the city stayed indoors. He worked a routine — keep the walkways clear, pull stray trash before it iced over — until a handbag near Hao Road in Xinjiekou pulled him off that route. It felt abandoned. When he opened it, he saw neat slices of cooked meat. The color and finish suggested pork. He took it home. Under a tap, piece by piece, he rinsed away grit. His hand closed on something rigid and unfamiliar. He pulled it free and saw a human finger. Two more lay among the meat. He stopped, called the police, and handed over the bag he had meant to turn into a stew.

Officers began with skepticism and then saw the same thing he had seen. No prank produced three human fingers. No ordinary household would discard so much prepared meat. The bag went straight to the station. Hours later, the examination result was plain: human remains.

Police widened their search. Around Nanjing University they found more, at the stadium, near the gate, outside a hospital, and along nearby roads. Each package had the same logic: plastic wrap; meat cut small; the look of cooked pork overlaying something else. Ten days later, clothing surfaced that investigators believed belonged to the victim. With mid-

44

1990s forensic tools, DNA was not practical in the way it is now, so they moved by accumulation. Muscle and hair provided limited markers, and clothing provided another set. The conclusion they reached was categorical: the victim was female. A name followed after outreach to families of missing persons and after a small mole on the right cheek helped confirm identity. The woman was Dao A-qing.

By the end of the initial sweep, the count of recovered fragments exceeded 2000. They were wrapped in plastic, distributed across multiple locations with a center of gravity near the university. The cuts were precise. The neck's dissection line was especially clean. Investigators concluded this was not amateur work. A butcher's hand, or a surgeon's, or at least someone with practiced familiarity with anatomy and a steady tolerance for the task.

One detail shaped both the investigation and the rumors that followed. Portions of the body had been cooked not once but over several days. That made time-of-death analysis less precise. It rendered the face unrecognizable. It destroyed some of the trace signatures investigators rely upon. And another fact pushed the case into a separate category of violence: the heart, liver, and spleen were missing.

Dao was born in March 1976 in Shanggao, Changyan District, Taizhou City, Jiangsu Province. She was the younger of two sisters. Her family's resources were limited. Winters required sharing a coat, and new clothes felt out of reach. Her older sister, Dao Ai-hua, left school to work so the younger sister could stay in class. Dao wanted to help as well but was told to study instead. In October 1995 she enrolled at Nanjing University's School of Adult Education, majoring in computer applications in the Department of Information Management. Her family could not send devices or extras. They kept losses and funerals to themselves so she could concentrate. Friends described her as introverted, orderly, and not given to display. She wore a small rotation of neat clothes, studied hard, and kept a narrow social circle for company when she needed it.

In early January 1996 she returned to her hometown for dinner with classmates, then came back to Nanjing the next day. On January 10, at about five p.m., classmates saw her leave the Gulou campus. In the hours before she walked out, a dormitory issue had flared: her roommate had used an induction cooker, a violation of rules. Dorm staff levied a fine and told Dao to pay half because the device had been used in her room. She objected but the staff did not yield. After that exchange, she left the building wearing a red coat with a black lining. It was exam week and her habit was to seal herself into study when pressure rose. Her bed was made before she left. Friends thought she might be taking a short break and would be back but she did not come back at all.

Her absence was reported to the dorm administration, which chose not to inform her family immediately. They limited the information to staff and a few students. Nine days later, the bag was found.

The first hours and days after identification built an investigative frame. The skill implied by the cuts suggested a person familiar with animals or bodies. The cooking suggested time in a place with a stove. The distribution suggested either an attempt to scatter attention or simply a practical means of disposal. Police considered the simplest profile that fit those elements. One internal outline, later described publicly, focused on a single, physically fit middle-aged man living alone with access to a kitchen. Officers searched the dorms and the perimeter that supported the campus, looking for someone who matched. Nothing came out of it.

A special task force set up inside the university worked for three months. The mid-1990s relied on paper ledgers and footwork. Public surveillance networks were rare. Buildings with cameras were the exception. The bags, the plastic wrap, and the handbag used to move the meat was ordinary. Even the printed bed sheet that later appeared in a police notice was ordinary enough that it did not single out a buyer. Officers canvassed students, staff, and teachers. They took statements, asked each student to account for the night Dao disappeared, then for the nights when bags were found. They sent notices to neighborhoods and to families of the missing, and asked for tips. Rumors ran in the space that evidence could not fill. The task force wound down when repeated passes over the same ground produced nothing new.

When a case resists resolution, theories multiply. Some began with the facts and widened their circle. Cooking, scattering, and removal of organs suggested an effort to erase traces and complicate identification. Others took the missing organs as a starting point and reached for broader systems. A widely repeated line of thought linked the case to the organ trade. A later paper by Xue Wang, cited in online discussions, described how executed prisoners had been a primary source of transplant organs since 1983 and how that system was officially abolished in 2015, leaving an even tighter supply. That pattern, plus the details of this case, made a fit that many found persuasive. No direct evidence supported the link. The theory persisted because it was comprehensive: it explained the missing organs, the skill, and the lack of a local suspect. Another group of discussions turned to cannibalism. That framing had a shock value that kept it alive in stories even when it made less sense of the logistics. If someone intended to eat, why leave so much behind? Scattering created witnesses. Silence would have been the easier path.

In the first months of the case, police released what they thought might prompt recognition: the kind of plastic bags, the model of handbag, the pattern on a bed sheet. They asked the public to look closely. Nothing returned that could be acted upon. Years later, the case took on a second life online. On March 21, 2007, a user named Shiliu Cha posted a detailed account. On May 28, 2008, anonymous users opened a "Dao A-qing bar" to collect what could be collected — press clippings, photos, routes, guesses. On June 19, a user with the name "Hey Misa" posted an analysis called "A Little Thought on the Nanjing Corpse Dismemberment Case," arguing that the killer likely knew Dao and might have been in love with her. The post spread widely and drew attention because it was organized and confident where most commentary was not. Some readers thought the author knew more than he claimed.

On June 24, 2008, Nanjing's Modern Express wrote about the online traffic. The police took interest. Shortly afterward, the "Hey Misa" posts disappeared. That absence provoked the usual conclusions. Later reporting said "Hey Misa" was a twenty-six-year-old male law student whose father had been a police officer, that he had agreed to cooperate if asked, and that his posts were largely speculation rather than evidence. Police asked the forum to remove the content; moderators complied. No arrest followed from those threads.

On July 4, 2008, a netizen using the name "Dao Hong Shuan" traveled at his own expense from Shandong to Nanjing and to Jiangyan, where he sought out Dao's parents. Her father received him. Her brother-in-law was wary and contacted the Jiangyan Public Security Bureau, which brought the visitor in for questioning. On July 13, after tips from other users, the same man wrote on his blog that a novelist, Wang Dain, whose 1998 book Jinyan Wu (The Memorial) had appeared two years after the killing, might be linked to the crime. The author publicly denied the claim, called it imaginative extrapolation built on rumors that had already been proven thin, and moved on. No formal action followed.

On January 19, 2016, a local WeChat account marked the date for a reason that had nothing to do with weather. Twenty years had passed since the remains were first recovered, the period that some read as the outer limit for prosecution. The message was stark: if the law's clock ran out, a confession would carry no legal consequence. The reaction was swift. The next afternoon, the Criminal Investigation Bureau of the Ministry of Public Security posted on Weibo that the case would continue to be investigated without an expiration date, and that it would be pursued to the end. Legal scholars argued over how statutes should apply in a case like this and how exceptions could be structured. The public message simplified the point. The work would continue.

In May 2022, a post on Weibo claimed the case was solved and tied that claim to an arrest in the separate Hulan police murder case. The link traveled quickly. It fit a pattern of hope and resolution that these cases attract. On May 30, the pattern collapsed. Dao's family, Nanjing police, and the Cyberspace Administration all said the rumor was false and that the case remained unsolved. The original poster was banned for spreading misinformation.

Nanjing University refunded Dao's tuition to her family. In March 2021, twenty-five years after the killing, Dao's sister filed a lawsuit in the Gulou District People's Court seeking 1.62 million yen in compensation, arguing that the university had failed to protect Dao, particularly after punishing her on January 10 and allowing her to leave alone, and pointing to the distribution of remains around campus as evidence that safety had not been adequately managed. A week later she withdrew the suit. No reason was made public. Dao's father visited the university four times over the years seeking updates, the last visit reported as either 2010 or 2022 depending on the source. During that visit, he requested assistance and received 10,000 yen after signing a letter promising not to seek further compensation connected to the case.

What the record cannot yet hold is a name. The suspect profiles have not matched a person the police could arrest and charge. The online energy has not delivered a lead the police could rely upon. The family's invitation to a hypothetical murderer — come forward, we will forgive — has not changed the silence. For those who study violent crime, this is a familiar shape: a limited set of physical facts, a narrowed set of possible motives, and a wide, durable field of interpretation that grows each time the date rolls around. At this point, even one person's choice to speak, or on a small, neglected detail found by someone patient enough to look again can bring so much to the light.

Yet, until that happens, the case remains what it has been for almost 30 years: a set of dates and places, a family that holds a name close, a university that still sits at the center of the map, and a winter story that began when a man on a late shift bent down to pick up a bag.

8

THE ORDER OF THE LION

In the pre-dawn darkness of May 21, 1990, a phone call shattered the quiet of Salida, California. At approximately 2:00 a.m., police were dispatched to a home on the corner of Mason and Elm Street, responding to a report of multiple murders. When officers arrived, they were confronted with a scene of incomprehensible brutality. They found the bodies of four victims: three men and one woman, later identified as thirty-five-year-old Dennis Colwell, twenty-five-year-old Richard Ritchie, fifty-one-year-old Franklin Raper, and twenty-three-year-old Darlene Paris. Raper, they would soon learn, was the owner of the home.

Amid the carnage, police located one survivor, a woman named Donna Alvarez. She was found in a state of profound shock, a blanket over her head, as if to block out the reality of what she had witnessed. As the attack began, Alvarez had managed to escape the main living area and ran into the garage. She burrowed under a pile of dirty clothes, remaining perfectly still until the sounds of violence subsided. When she believed the attackers were gone, she pried open the garage door, slipped out, and ran to a neighbor's house to call for help.

Donna told the officers she had been staying at Franklin Raper's home, a courtesy he often extended to those with nowhere else to go. She had been introduced to Raper by one of the other victims, Richard Ritchie. Her account of the attack was chaotic and terrifying. She said a group of people, all wearing camouflage, had burst into the house simultaneously through doors and windows, immediately assaulting everyone inside. She noted one man in particular, a white male in his mid-twenties, about six feet tall (about 182 centimeters), who was not wearing a mask and was holding a silver gun. His most distinct feature, she told them, was his afro-like hair.

This specific description stood out to the officers on the scene. While surveying the area, a detective noticed a local lingering nearby. The detective approached him and asked if he knew anyone who matched that description. He identified the person as "Jason," a man who lived at a place known locally as "the Camp."

The Camp, detectives learned, was an old labor camp now occupied by people living in campers and trailers. Neighbors of the Camp filled in more details. They told police the people living there were involved in some kind of weird military group and had a reputation for intimidating the people who lived there. The neighbors provided names: Gerald Cruz, David Beck, Ricky Vieira, and the man Donna had described, Jason LaMarsh.

The most critical piece of information came when the neighbors told police that one of the victims, Franklin Raper, had recently lived at the Camp himself. He had left after a major falling out with the other men and moved to the house on Elm Street. Suddenly, the investigation had a direct link between the victims and a secretive, militaristic group. Before heading to the Camp, detectives ran Jason LaMarsh's name through their system. He had a prior record, which meant they had a photo. They presented a lineup to Donna Alvarez, who immediately identified Jason LaMarsh as the unmasked attacker.

Armed with a positive identification, detectives drove to the Camp. No one was there, but the property itself offered immediate clues. They saw a small studio house toward the back of the property and, hanging on a clothesline, freshly washed camouflage clothing that matched Donna's description. As the officers were preparing to leave, a car pulled up. The driver, Gerald Cruz, got out and was met by the detectives. Cruz was perfectly calm, telling police he knew nothing about any murders. Before leaving to secure a search warrant, they asked him to confirm the names of the other residents. He listed David Beck, Jason LaMarsh, and Ricky Vieira.

With the warrant in hand, police returned and began a methodical search of the property. What they found inside the small house belonging to Gerald Cruz and his wife, Jennifer, began to paint a disturbing picture of the man who lived there. They discovered bomb-making materials, military manuals, and satanic literature, including *The Satanic Bible*. They also found a copy of *The Big Book of Secret Hiding Places*, a guide for concealing contraband. And then they found two items that provided a chilling glimpse into the group's internal dynamics: a strange wooden wheel divided into sections, each bearing a different form of punishment, and a collection of journals.

These journals, police realized, were the key. They contained disturbing entries that detailed the life of the group at the Camp, confirming the suspicions of the investigators. This was not just a military group; it was a cult, and Gerald Cruz was its leader.

Gerald Dean Cruz was born Gerald Dean Cox in Modesto, California, around March of 1962. His entire life was shrouded in confusion about his parentage. He was raised believing his mother was a woman named Hortencia Cruz and his father was Ascencio Cruz. Ascencio, however, had returned to Mexico before Gerald was born, unaware Hortencia was pregnant. In his absence, Hortencia listed a friend, Lawrence Cox, on the birth certificate. When Ascencio returned to Modesto two years later, he was shocked to learn he had a son.

Gerald grew up with the surname Cruz, but when he entered school, he was called Gerald Cox. This was how he learned of the discrepancy on his birth certificate, fueling a lifelong confusion. The truth was elusive; family members who testified at his trial years later gave conflicting accounts of his childhood. One half-sister, Marlene, claimed that Hortencia was not his mother at all. She testified that Gerald's real mother was Hope, another woman believed to be his older half-sister, and that his father was, in fact, Lawrence Cox.

According to Marlene, who was fourteen when Gerald was born, his childhood was one of severe abuse. She described Hortencia as a violent woman who was cruel to animals and children alike. Marlene and Hope, who apparently fought over whose responsibility it was to care for Gerald, would allegedly beat him with switches, ropes, electrical cords, umbrellas, and hangers.

This trauma at home was mirrored by torment at school. Gerald was bullied relentlessly for his clothes and his hair, and for the fact that he did not know who his real father was. This search for identity became a defining struggle. Experts who later studied him suggested that this void drove him to invent an identity for himself. He began to believe he was special, that he possessed special powers and abilities. These delusions, born from a childhood of abuse and confusion, morphed as he grew older, emerging in a sadistic desire for control.

Gerald's beliefs were eclectic and ever-changing, a hallmark of what psychologists would later call a "cult of personality." The group's doctrine was not fixed; it was simply whatever Gerald willed it to be. One moment he was focused on white supremacy and the idea of a "master race," the next he was immersed in black magic, the occult, and satanism. The only constant was his own authority. Having failed to succeed in mainstream society, he had withdrawn and, as one psychologist noted, "collected around himself a band of people almost like a Neanderthal clan."

He preyed on the vulnerable: the homeless, the lost, those disconnected from their families. He offered them a place to stay, the promise of a family, and a sense of belonging. For a short time, life for a new member would be good. But once Gerald sensed their complete psychological and physical dependence, his true nature would emerge.

By his early twenties, Gerald was living in a home in Modesto when he met Ricky Vieira. Ricky, likely fifteen or sixteen at the time, was a perfect target. He came from a terrible home life, abused by his father and neglected by his mother. He was desperate for an escape, and Gerald swooped in, offering him a home, a "family," and a new path. Ricky moved into Gerald's home, and for a little while, he felt he finally belonged.

Around the same time, in the mid-1980s, two of Gerald's childhood friends re-entered his life and became core members of the group. David Beck, who had known Gerald for years, had drifted away, gotten married, found success in his career, and become a devoutly religious man. But after a difficult divorce, Beck was lost. He reconnected with Gerald and soon became his second-in-command. Beck's family would later say he became a different person, changing from a happy, bubbly man into a withdrawn, zombie-like figure. Another old friend, Ron Willey, also reconnected with Gerald and Beck, getting drawn into the periphery of the emerging cult.

Another early recruit, Stephen Perkins, moved in around the same time as Ricky Vieira. With his inner circle formed, Gerald began to formalize his control. He gave the men journals — the same ones police would later find — and instructed them to write in them constantly. They were to detail their deepest fears, insecurities, and thoughts. Gerald would read their entries and use their vulnerabilities against them. He kept his own journal, in which he made the men cut their hands and leave a bloody fingerprint as a binding contract of their devotion.

He initiated weekly ceremonies where the men would dress in white robes resembling Ku Klux Klan (KKK) attire, light candles, chant, and speak in gibberish. The group's ideology was a chaotic mix of religion, military structure, and the occult. Almost immediately, the psychological control escalated to physical abuse. Gerald would make Ricky and Stephen stand perfectly still in a room while he punched them in the stomach as hard as he could. On at least one occasion, he struck Stephen Perkins with such force that the man required hospitalization. He also used a scorpion stun gun on them for his own amusement.

David Beck, his right-hand man, was the only one exempt from the abuse; in fact, he often participated in it. Together, Gerald and Beck would inflict a torture they called the "Orange Line Treatment." They would cut an orange extension cord, attach the severed end to a man's foot with duct tape, and plug the cord into an outlet wired to a light switch. Gerald would then flip the switch, sending electrical shocks through the man's body while he and Beck laughed. This "treatment" was inflicted on

Stephen Perkins so severely that his foot turned black and became badly infected.

In 1987, the twenty-five-year-old Gerald began dating sixteen-year-old Jennifer Starn. She soon moved into the Modesto home with Gerald, Stephen, and Ricky. Gerald made no effort to hide the abuse from her; he beat the men openly in front of her, and soon, he began abusing her as well. When she angered him, he would put a gun in her mouth. Jennifer quickly became pregnant twice, and the presence of two infants in the home did nothing to curb Gerald's violence. When she was two months pregnant with one of the children, he pushed her to the ground and repeatedly kicked her in the stomach, causing her to bleed. She fled barefoot to a women's shelter but stayed only four days before Gerald found her and convinced her to return.

His cruelty extended to his own children. Court documents detail the systematic abuse of his infant daughter, referred to as "Baby A." As a form of punishment, Gerald would place the six-month-old in a dark room by herself, permitting Jennifer to enter only every six hours, but not to hold or console the child. When Baby A made him angry, he would strike her on the legs with a fly swatter or a ruler. He built a contraption he called "the rack," from which he would suspend the baby in a harness. He would then attach mason jars full of water to her legs and intentionally make her cry, causing her to instinctively kick against the weights. He would also slap her hard on the side of the head, an act he called "a clapping," sometimes hitting her with enough force to cause bruising inside her ears. When she was learning to walk, he would ask her if she "wanted a clapping," and the terrified child would immediately drop to the ground and hide her head. Other members of the group participated. On one occasion, Gerald, Beck, and Vieira placed a tape recorder next to Baby A's crib, waited for her to drift off to sleep, and then screamed as loud as they could to startle her. They recorded her hysterical crying which Jennifer later played in court.

In late 1989, Gerald, Jennifer, and their children moved to the Camp, setting up in the small house on the property. Ricky Vieira came with them, moving into an adjacent trailer. Stephen Perkins, however, did not. The seventeen months he had spent with Gerald had destroyed him.

When he returned to his parents' home, he was a different person. He had lost 125 pounds (about fifty-six kilograms) and was moody and withdrawn, refusing to speak to anyone. His foot was severely infected from the Orange Line Treatments, and he had broken bones from the beatings. Gerald had warned him to tell no one, instructing him to claim he'd been in a motorcycle accident. Stephen developed severe claustrophobia and mental lapses, forgetting the day of the week. He became suicidal and eventually admitted himself to a psychiatric hospital.

With Stephen gone, Ricky Vieira became the primary target of Gerald's sadism. Gerald began using the "Will of Punishment," the wooden wheel police found during the search. He would force a member to throw the wheel in the air and catch it; whatever punishment their thumb landed on was their fate. Punishments included eating off the floor, solitary confinement, and severe beatings. The abuse also escalated to sexual assault, with Gerald forcing the men to sodomize each other in front of the group.

Soon after the move to the Camp, Jason LaMarsh and Franklin Raper arrived. Jason, who had only known the group for a few months before the murders, quickly fell in with them. Franklin Raper, however, was an outcast. No one in the group liked him. The conflict began when LaMarsh, who was sharing a trailer with Raper, woke up to find his pants pocket cut and his gun missing. He immediately blamed Raper, and from that day on, he hated him, complaining about him constantly to Gerald.

Gerald claimed he disliked Raper for being a drug user who left needles lying around. The men fought constantly, until Gerald finally told Raper to move his trailer off the property. When Raper refused, Gerald waited for him to leave, hooked the trailer to a car, and towed it off the property. He and his followers then filled Raper's car with his belongings, pushed it across the street, and set it on fire.

This act forced Franklin Raper to relocate. He moved into the house on Elm Street, a property that was already connected to the cult. The house belonged to Tanya, the sister of Jason LaMarsh's girlfriend, Michelle Evans. Even though Gerald had gotten his wish and Raper was gone, it wasn't enough. He decided that Franklin Raper needed to die.

The morning before the murders, Michelle Evans needed to retrieve some furniture from the Elm Street house. She asked Gerald, Jason, and the others to help her, knowing Franklin Raper would be there. A fight quickly broke out between LaMarsh and Raper. The group left after only forty-five minutes and returned to the Camp, but the confrontation had solidified Gerald's resolve.

That night, Gerald gathered his followers (David Beck, Ricky Vieira, Jason LaMarsh, and Ron Willey) in LaMarsh's trailer. Michelle Evans was also present. Gerald told them they were going to the house on Elm Street to kill Franklin Raper. His orders were explicit: they were to kill everyone there, leaving no witnesses. He knew Raper often let people stay with him, and he was prepared for collateral damage.

Michelle Evans's job was to draw a blueprint of the house, marking all doors and windows. She was also instructed to go in first, to gather everyone in the living room to make the attack easier. Gerald also had her call her sister, Tanya, and tell her not to go home that night.

On the night of May 20, 1990, the group held a barbecue at the Camp, doing drugs, listening to heavy metal music, and swinging bats and batons to "pump themselves up." Just after midnight, on May 21, Gerald Cruz, Jason LaMarsh, Ricky Vieira, David Beck, and Ron Willey piled into a car and headed for Franklin's house. They were armed with knives, batons, and bats. All wore camouflage clothing and masks, except for Jason LaMarsh and Michelle Evans. LaMarsh also carried his gun.

The cult members parked down the street. Michelle Evans and Jason LaMarsh got out and approached the house. Michelle went in first, likely without raising suspicion, and unlocked a window. Donna Alvarez was asleep in a bedroom when Michelle woke her, telling her she needed to get up because Tanya needed the room. Donna gathered her things and walked into the living room, where Raper was sitting in a chair. As she and Richard Ritchie headed toward another bedroom, Beck and Vieira burst in through the unlocked window, followed immediately by the rest of the men.

As the attack began, Michelle Evans walked out the front door, returned to the car, and waited. As she left, she could hear Darlene Paris screaming and pleading for her life. Amid the chaos, Donna Alvarez slipped away unnoticed and hid in the garage.

Jason LaMarsh went straight for Franklin Raper, beating him with a baton as he sat in his chair. Raper tried to shield himself with his arms, but LaMarsh struck him with such force that it broke his arm. He beat Raper relentlessly until his face was unrecognizable, then pulled out a knife and slit his throat.

While this was happening, Gerald and the other men were attacking Dennis Colwell and Richard Ritchie. Darlene Paris, watching the horror unfold, was screaming. Annoyed, Gerald looked at Ricky Vieira and ordered, "Shut her up." Vieira grabbed Darlene by the hair, pulled her head back, and began cutting at her throat. He didn't stop until he felt the blade hit bone.

One of the victims, Richard Ritchie, managed to escape the house and staggered onto the front lawn. Gerald Cruz and Ron Willey chased him down, beat him brutally, and cut his throat in full view of neighbors who were watching in shock from their homes.

When the police investigation led them back to the Camp, the arrests began. Gerald and Jennifer were taken into custody for the bomb-making materials. David Beck and Ricky Vieira were quickly located. Detectives sensed Vieira was the weak link. As a technician was hooking him up for a polygraph test, Ricky broke. "Okay," he said, "I guess I should probably tell you that I killed Darlene Paris." Jason LaMarsh had already fled the state but was arrested a week later in an Oregon motel after a friend he was traveling with, to whom he had confessed, called the police.

At trial, the full, horrific details of the murders were laid bare. The autopsies confirmed the brutality of the attack. Dennis Colwell had a skull fracture and multiple stab wounds, and his throat was cut. Franklin Raper's head was so badly beaten that his skull was fragmented, and his throat was also cut. Richard Ritchie had been stabbed in the neck, back, abdomen, liver, and heart. Darlene Paris had been beaten and stabbed, but her cause of death was the wound to her throat, which was so deep it cut down to her spine, nearly decapitating her. Her mother later said she was forced to bury her daughter in a turtleneck.

Gerald Cruz, David Beck, and Ricky Vieira were all convicted of first-degree murder and sentenced to death. They remain on death row. Jason LaMarsh was convicted of second-degree murder and sentenced to sixty-four years to life. Ron Willey's outcome was not specified in the reports. Michelle Evans, for her part in drawing the blueprint and setting the stage for the massacre, took a plea deal. In exchange for her testimony, she was found guilty of being an accessory and served only six months in prison.

Ricky Vieira continues to appeal his conviction, arguing that he was completely brainwashed by Gerald Cruz and participated only because he feared for his life. For the victims, justice was partial and complicated. Franklin Raper was a grandfather. Dennis Colwell, Richard Ritchie, and Darlene Paris were guilty of nothing more than being in the wrong place at the wrong time, their lives ended in an eruption of violence orchestrated by one man's sadistic need for absolute control.

9

ÇIFTLIK BANK SCAM

Imagine a young man born in 1991, raised in a country where graduation from top schools is supposed to be the ticket into a decent life but isn't. His peers spend years at İTÜ (İstanbul Teknik Üniversitesi), METU (Middle East Technical University), Boğaziçi — engineering, business, social sciences — only to discover that the jobs waiting for them often come with managers who can't form a clean sentence and pay offers barely above the minimum. The cycle is familiar and dispiriting. Into that landscape steps a boyish face with a grin that reads as confidence to some and condescension to others. He would, in time, be listed by Interpol. He would be called a prodigy by a few and a con man by many more.

The man's name is Mehmet Aydın. The enterprise he gave to the public imagination was Çiftlik Bank. What follows is the shape of that story as it was told to his audience and as participants later told it back — dates, names, amounts, and the reasons people offered for why they trusted him.

Aydın's family traces back to Giresun; they moved to Bursa, where he attended an imam-hatip high school (a religion focused high school) and left before completing it. He washed dishes in a café for minimum wage. On the side he tested small online hustles, including selling bet slips through a website. He loved rap, posted tracks under stage names — "Eren Çakar," "egomen" — and taught himself enough software to tinker.

None of that made him rich, but it gave him two ingredients he would use later: a feel for how to set up a website people can pay into, and a knack for telling an audience what it wants to hear.

By mid-2016 he had the framework of an idea: take the familiar pleasure loop of a farm game and couple it to real money. He could sketch the logic but not build the whole thing alone, so he pulled in a programmer he knew. The coder wasn't a star — just competent enough to make things work. Their relationship soured; in later accounts the programmer said he walked away and that even his fee had been shaved — asked for 1,000 liras (about twenty-four dollars today), got paid half. Whether that was an omen or a footnote, the pattern people later described was already visible.

On July 31, 2016, the Çiftlik Bank game went live.

It did not take long for the first test of trust. A sixteen-year-old deposited 4,000 liras (about 100 dollars today). In the following days, intake climbed to about 20,000 liras (about 500 dollars) a day. At first, the money flowed straight into his personal bank account — an amateur choice that signaled both naivety and urgency. Personal accounts draw attention when the numbers swell, and they don't look professional to someone considering an "investment." To make incoming funds look more like a business and less like a man with a bank card, he began taking payments through Papara. Within a month — September 2, 2016 — he created a company with a name designed to radiate both tech and agriculture: "Çiftlik Bilgi İşlem Bilişim Tarım ve Hayvancılık Limited Şirketi." The paid-in capital was 10,000 liras (about 250 dollars today). He was the founder.

From there, the circle widened. He brought in relatives and trusted contacts. As the operation grew more technical, he recruited "experts," in software and in agriculture, to stand beside the brand and lend it the right vocabulary. The storytelling goal was simple: a modern enterprise running on code and cows.

The internal economy was built to be simple. Deposit 10,000 liras (about 250 dollars today), receive 10,000 units of in-game "gold." This "gold" was only a name, not pegged to market precious metals, and it remained inside the system at a fixed 1:1 with the lira. A second currency — "silver"

— had a specific use: retail purchases at Çiftlik-branded delicatessens. Players were encouraged to spend time and money inside the game loop: buy animals, buy feed, buy embryos, rent storage, keep the cycle running. Animals had lifespans; inputs had prices; outputs generated revenue. New users received a free "Manisa chicken," a small gift meant to soften the first step across the threshold.

Gross income was calculated by the system; feed and other costs were deducted to produce a net. Five percent of the income was automatically converted into silver. If you made 10,000 liras (about 250 dollars today), 500 liras (about twelve dollar today) of that would appear as silver in your account, something you could spend at the company's delis. The mechanics created a rhythm: you "invest" by buying animals; you "earn" as they produce; part of that earning becomes store credit redeemable in the brand's retail network.

The deli layer mattered because it gave people something to point to. Anyone — member or not — could walk into a Çiftlik Bank delicatessen, a grocery that sells a selection of fine prepared foods, and buy cheese, honey, butter, sausage. Members, however, could settle part of the bill with silver. Franchise owners, according to people in the system, even received more for a silver transaction than a cash one — ten to twenty percent more, roughly. That detail did double work: it nudged members to shop there, and it convinced owners they were in a business with guaranteed foot traffic as the user base grew.

Some who entered as players decided the "real money" was in the storefronts and opened delis. There were conditions: standardized interiors; opening events; buses arranged from other branches to make a show of crowds. The brand took a franchise fee that rose as the network expanded. The message to the street was clear: this wasn't only an online game; it was a physical network of shops and "farms."

The more visible the network became, the more central Aydın seemed. Franchisees described WhatsApp groups where he was active, available to answer questions and to manage anxieties when rumors began to swirl. When trouble came — arguments about backdoors in the code, missing funds, managers accused of theft — he told franchise owners that internal saboteurs had hurt him too. The tone wasn't fearmongering but rather marshaling, saying: Stay in. We're solving it.

There were claims that even land purchases were padded — plots valued at one number recorded at double to skim the difference. Whether that enriched insiders or middlemen, the effect was the same: bleed the pool while the pool was full. None of it appeared to slow the expansion. The impression he needed to keep alive was that money, land, animals, and inventory were all moving in the right direction. Speed and optics mattered more than efficiency.

Three pillars of trust supported the growth. The first was liquidity — at least early on. Users could withdraw on demand. Skeptics tested the system with 1000 liras (about twenty-five dollars today), saw 1,200 liras (about thirty dollars today) a month later, and pulled it out. That receipt was convertible into persuasion: friends showed each other bank statements. The next step was intuitive — 10,000 liras (about 250 dollars today) turn into 12,000 liras (about 300 dollars today); then 100,000 liras (about 2.500 dollars today) become 120,000 liras (about 3,000 dollars today). If you didn't have that much cash, you borrowed, sold a car, sold a house. The interest cost felt irrelevant if the principal multiplied on schedule. People told themselves they'd upgrade the car next month.

The second pillar was the presence of a product. The delis existed. The shelves were stocked. People bought food. Ministry inspections of food establishments happen in Turkey; the mere fact that a deli door was open and stocked persuaded some that all of this must be under official eyes. The staged openings of "facilities" amplified the impression: if a governor, a district governor, or a mayor cuts a ribbon, how fraudulent could it be?

The third pillar was the use of recognizable faces and mass-market airtime. Celebrities fronted ads. Openings featured familiar hosts. Commercials ran across channels, including a heavily watched program, "Beyaz Show," where the promo copy promised facilities in Sakarya, Manisa, Tekirdağ, Kırklareli built to European standards. If you already liked and trusted the presenter, that confidence bled into the brand. None of this, by itself, proves a company sound; all of it, together, can quiet questions.

Behind the glass, the supply chain was more prosaic. The cheeses, honeys, butters, and sausages came from existing producers under contract and private label. A Bursa company called Feyza made kashar; other goods were filled in by different suppliers, including in İstanbul's Kağıthane. The "farms," as multiple people later described them, were built for demonstration value. One detail from a call-in segment on a daytime program captured the logic: animals purchased for a facility didn't match the stated agricultural plan, but the orders went through anyway. The priority was a look, not a yield.

That raises the questions so few asked in time: if a hundred people each bought a cow in the game, where were the hundred real cows? What ratio existed between virtual inventory and live animals? How were in-game prices set? A cow priced at a token figure on a screen bears no relation to market price. None of those mismatches derailed the story.

Faces mattered. Actor Mehmet Çevik became the front man in ads and a recurring presence at openings, later saying he had no intent to lend cover to a deception and apologizing to those who felt misled. Another recognizable figure was Cengiz Çimen — "Mülayim" from daytime TV — familiar to older audiences. "Fısfıs İsmail" (İsmail Yaşar) from "Çocuklar Duymasın" surfaced, too. The creative strategy for some commercials was almost anti-creative: so bad they stick. Lines you mock are lines you remember. As for program-integrated placement, the "Beyaz Show" promo was the apex: a trusted host's voice and platform describing the company's facilities as modern and hygienic. On paper, none of that constitutes due diligence; in practice, it looked like certification.

Layered onto the spectacle were occasional appeals to religion and public feeling — references to Jerusalem at openings, for instance — content with no material link to the business but a clear aim: align the brand with values and causes ordinary people care about.

It took time for formal complaints to catch up. In May 2017, a first tip reached the Bursa Chief Public Prosecutor. On July 31, 2017, Aydın gave a statement to police. He said the company operated three farms — Manisa, İnegöl, Tekirdağ — with roughly 100,000 live animals: 95,000 chickens and the remainder cattle, including a breed that laid "blue eggs." The blue egg hook was everywhere: a planned breeding facility, claims that the protein content was one-and-a-half times that of a normal egg, an ambition to build the world's largest blue-egg operation. He said the company had granted twenty deli distributorships, booked annual turnover of fifteen million liras (about 360,000 dollars today) on a four-million profit (about 95,000 dollars today), and was US-registered under a parent called "Fame Game." At that moment, officials didn't have documents disproving his claims; the surface still looked orderly.

In December 2017, the ownership picture shifted. Aydın transferred company shares to a Cypriot company controlled by his brother, Fatih Aydın. The Capital Markets Board filed a criminal complaint. The Ministry of Customs and Trade accused the organization of aggravated fraud. New member registrations stopped. The engine shuddered.

On January 2, Aydın tried to normalize the transfer: the virtual activities and the physical delis had been merged under the "Fame Game" umbrella, he said. He repeated points about doing in the real world what the game simulated. He noted that their work was being examined by the ministry. Twenty two days later, on January 24, 2018, he left the country without incident.

The Anadolu Chief Public Prosecutor's Office would later present the system's outline in numbers. More than half a million people joined; not all put in money. About 188,099 played only as gamers. Around 132,222 deposited funds and became victims. The flows were stark: roughly 1.12 billion liras (about twenty-four million dollars today) came in; 687 million liras (about sixteen million dollars today) went back out. Early withdrawals and ongoing liquidity explain that give-and-take. The difference offers a crude measure of loss, though it cannot capture distribution: some withdrew more than they put in, which necessarily means others bore more than their share of the deficit. Press coverage often cited 77,000 people defrauded of 511 million liras (about twelve million dollars today).

How did that money leave the country? The claims ranged from suitcase cash to structured transfers. If he converted a large share into dollars at exit, the arithmetic worked in his favor. Allegations also surfaced about networks: suggestions of ties to Gülen movement, an Islamist fraternal movement, through land purchases; reports that an Uruguayan businessman from Bursa's Kestel district, Osman Aykaç, handled construction and laundering. They remained allegations in the public telling; what mattered to victims was simpler — their money was gone.

The stories that linger come from people who thought they were stepping into a sure thing. Some tested with small amounts and stopped while others took loans, sold cars, sold houses and went in heavy. When the music stopped, a few were drawn into a second humiliation: self-styled "recovery" agents demanded 500 (about twelve dollars today) to 1,000 liras (about twenty-five dollars today) in cash from 1,650 people, promising to get their losses back. They disappeared, too.

The human need to believe ran straight through it all. A deli franchisee told a newspaper he still refused to see Aydın as a swindler, pointing to his humble background and "sparkle" when opening companies. That sentiment — "he's one of us; a modest boy" — survived footage of him living well after the collapse. It is hard to argue with grief, but it is important to see the mechanism: attachment to a person can override evidence.

What remains are lessons people claim they already knew and yet ignored: if returns are guaranteed, they are not honest. If a business must wrap itself in celebrity, spectacle, and borrowed legitimacy, it is selling confidence rather than value. If a "bank" lives only on a website and a storefront franchise, it is not a bank. And if a system begins by proving it will pay you quickly, that may not be proof of soundness — it may be bait.

10

"SHE'S FIGHTING!"

Thirty-seven-year-old Jimmy Allen, who, just eighteen minutes earlier, had discovered his wife's body hanging from the ceiling in the basement of their home in Michigan frantically called 911. He told the dispatcher he had found her and was trying to perform CPR. As instructed, he continued his efforts while emergency units raced to the scene. Officer Ben J. Horn was the first to arrive, and as he approached the residence, he was struck by an unnerving silence that stood in stark contrast to the desperation in Jimmy's voice on the call. The moment Officer Horn made his presence known, however, the silence was shattered by Jimmy's cries for help.

Inside, the officer found Jimmy in the basement, sobbing over the unresponsive body of his wife, Amy, as he continued chest compressions. He claimed she couldn't have been down for more than twenty minutes. A brief inspection of Amy's body revealed no significant injuries, only a very faint mark near her jugular. By 8:57 p.m., more officers and several Emergency Medical Technicians (EMTs) had arrived, descending into the basement to take over the life-saving efforts. Freed from the task, Jimmy's grief appeared to overwhelm him. He dramatically ripped off his shirt and collapsed onto the basement floor in a heap of emotion. Yet, just as quickly, he composed himself and watched the EMTs work on his wife.

This rapid oscillation between complete composure and theatrical emotional outbursts would become a recurring pattern throughout the night.

When an officer asked him to come upstairs, Jimmy calmly walked up the basement stairs, but upon entering the kitchen, he unleashed a sudden burst of rage on a bowl of potato chips, sending them scattering. The officers were unsure what to make of his erratic behavior as they tried to piece together the events of the evening. Jimmy provided a summary of the night, explaining that he and Amy had dropped their daughter and her friend off at a high school football game around 6:30 p.m. before heading downtown for drinks. While at a bar, an argument erupted, which resulted in Amy walking home alone while he drove. He said the arguing continued when they both got home, so he left her alone to cool off and went upstairs to watch the movie *Ace Ventura*. When it was time to pick up their daughter, he went to check on Amy and found her. He insisted that Amy had no history of anything like this and that he was completely shocked by the situation.

As the officers absorbed his story, an EMT emerged from the basement with an unexpected development. Amy was fighting; they had reestablished a faint pulse. She was still clinging to life. Instead of relief, Jimmy's reaction to this promising news appeared to be one of frustration, a response that immediately raised red flags for the officers on the scene. After momentarily leaving the room to get a new shirt, Jimmy returned and made two phone calls. The first was to his daughter, Ashley, whom he told there was an emergency and to stay put, keeping his composure to avoid panicking her. The second call was to his parents, and his demeanor shifted entirely as he spilled his heart out in a flood of emotion. Though he was crying intensely, an officer noted that there was no moisture on his face.

Shortly after, Amy was placed on a stretcher and rushed to Promedica Herrick Hospital, just two minutes away. With the basement now clear, officers began a more thorough investigation of the scene. One detail immediately stood out: the basement ceilings were unusually low, roughly seven feet high (about 2.13 meters). Given that Amy was five feet, six inches tall (about 1.67 meters), the logistics of Jimmy's implied narrative began to seem questionable.

The next morning, officers returned to the Allen home to speak with Jimmy again, hoping to get a clearer picture of the day leading up to the incident. Jimmy described a perfectly normal family day, starting with making breakfast together before he left for work and Ashley left for school. He came home from work early, around 12:30 p.m., and took a nap. Amy picked up Ashley and her friend Kayla from school, and the group had dinner together before leaving for the football game at 6:30 p.m.. From there, Jimmy and Amy went bar hopping, first to Embers Bar and Grill, and then to JR's Hometown Grill and Pub, a detail investigators later confirmed with security footage.

According to Jimmy, the trouble began at JR's when he brought up the idea of selling their house and moving back south to Florida, from where they had moved only a year prior. Amy was not receptive to the idea. She became dismissive, texting someone on her phone and responding negatively to his suggestions. He recalled her saying, "I hope that works out for you," a comment that sparked a tense argument. The tension was so thick by the time they left that Amy chose to walk home rather than ride with him. Surveillance footage confirmed this, capturing Amy walking in the direction of their house.

Jimmy stated that Amy arrived home at 7:58 p.m., grabbed an extension cord, and went to the basement. He went down to check on her at 8:05 p.m. and found her feeding one of their cats. She was angry with him, accusing him of slamming a door in her face as they left the bar, an act he insisted was an accident. They argued for another ten minutes before he went back upstairs, leaving her in the basement with the cord. At 8:40 p.m., realizing it was time to get their daughter, he went down to make peace with Amy and discovered the scene. He mentioned seeing an overturned kitty litter pail nearby when he found her. He maintained that he could never have seen this coming, describing their life as healthy and financially stable, the pinnacle of his career.

The officers' view of the Allen family began to shift dramatically when several of Amy's relatives approached them. They were concerned that Jimmy had waited fourteen hours to inform them of what had happened. They told investigators a story that painted Jimmy not as a shocked and grieving husband, but as a deeply controlling man. They explained that Amy had a son, Caleb, from a previous relationship when she was thirteen. Jimmy had initially acted as a father figure to Caleb, but the family dynamic was toxic. Amy's family claimed Jimmy monitored everything the family did, from social media to their daily diet, and that he didn't want Amy to be financially independent. His discipline of the children often went too far, and Amy's attempts to stand up to him were dismissed. Eventually, the environment became so unbearable that when Caleb was seventeen, he left to live with his grandparents. In retaliation, Jimmy forbade Amy from speaking with her family, including her son.

This portrait of an abusive and controlling husband provided a potential context for violence, but investigators still lacked a clear motive. That changed when they examined Amy's cell phone. Her text history with Jimmy confirmed his controlling behavior; he frequently texted her asking for her exact location, which he appeared to be tracking. The motive, however, was found in another conversation. Amy had been having a three-year-long affair with a married man from the East Coast named George, whom she had met online. Their messages were explicit, and they had been in constant contact on the day of the incident, texting and calling even while she was at dinner with her family. At the bar, while sitting next to her husband and arguing with him, she had been texting George. A new, powerful theory emerged: Jimmy had seen the texts, and in a fit of rage, attacked Amy in the basement.

Before investigators could follow up on this new lead, they received tragic news. On September 17, 2018, after three days on life support, Amy Allen was pronounced dead. The case was now a homicide investigation. However, when police tried to locate Jimmy for more questioning, they discovered he was gone. Just days after the incident, he had packed up his daughter, their five cats, and all their belongings and moved back to his hometown of Ocala, Florida.

The Michigan State Police took over the investigation, and one month after Amy's death, Detective Larry Rothman arranged for Jimmy to return for a formal interview. During the interview, Jimmy presented himself as a "type A personality" who valued structure and was always seeking to improve himself and his family. He framed his obsession with creating a perfect family as a strength, believing it was his role to hold them to a higher standard. He painted Amy as a socially anxious introvert who had isolated herself with a video game addiction, casting himself as the savior trying to help her break out of her shell. When Detective Rothman bluntly informed him that Amy had been having an affair, Jimmy was in complete denial. Even after being shown excerpts of her explicit conversations with George, he struggled to accept it.

Three months after Amy's death, the autopsy report was released. The cause of death was confirmed as strangulation asphyxiation, but the manner of death was listed as undetermined, pending further investigation. Detective Rothman, recalling the low basement ceiling, contacted a forensic engineering lab and asked them to recreate the scene. After months of testing, the lab concluded that, given the circumstances described, Amy's feet would have touched the ground. With this new evidence, a different forensic pathologist reviewed the case and determined the manner of death was homicide. On October 16, 2020, Jimmy Allen was charged with one felony count of open murder. He was arrested in Florida just five days before his wedding to his new fiancée and was extradited back to Michigan.

In September 2021, three years after Amy's death, Jimmy's trial began. The prosecution, led by Angie Borders, argued that Jimmy was a controlling husband who snapped after discovering his wife's affair. They called Amy's son, Caleb, who testified that Jimmy had choked him during an argument years earlier, suggesting a history of using strangulation when angry. First responders and a hospital staff member testified that Jimmy's over-the-top emotional displays seemed fake and that the lack of external injuries on Amy's body was a red flag for foul play. The prosecution's star witness was George, who took the stand to detail his three-year affair with Amy, confirming they had met in person twice, once in a hotel room, and were making plans to meet again at the end of October. Finally, Dr. Elizabeth Buck presented the results of the forensic experiment, testifying that the extension cord in question could not have suspended a 140-pound weight (about sixty-three kilograms), effectively debunking Jimmy's story.

The defense, led by attorney Daniel Garin, countered that the prosecution's case was built on speculation. They pointed to Jimmy's phone search history from that night — which included searches for Jim Carrey movies — as evidence that murder was not on his mind. Jimmy's father testified that the family had urged him to move to Florida after the tragedy, explaining his departure from the state. In a significant shift from her initial statement, Ashley testified that her mother frequently overindulged in alcohol and would become "meaner and more violent" when intoxicated. The defense argued that Amy's blood alcohol content of 0.09% was evidence of a drinking problem. They also brought in their own expert, Dr. Francisco J. Diaz, who testified that the minimal internal injuries to Amy's neck were inconsistent with a homicide. In his closing argument, Garin emphasized that Jimmy had no defensive scratches on him and portrayed Amy as a deeply troubled woman living a double life, whose isolation, drinking, and guilt over her affair ultimately led to her tragic death.

After six hours of deliberation, the jury reached a verdict. They found Jimmy Allen guilty of the lesser offense of second-degree murder. On October 21, 2021, he was sentenced to twenty to forty-five years in the Michigan Department of Corrections with an eligibility for parole in the year 2040.

On the surface, Jimmy Allen had presented himself as a grieving husband, a man caught in a tragic and unforeseeable moment. But beneath the veneer of composure and orchestrated emotion lay a history of control, manipulation, and escalating violence. The combination of forensic evidence, digital trails, and testimony from those closest to Amy ultimately unraveled the story he tried so hard to control. In the end, the tragic unraveling of a family's private life left a permanent mark on those who survived, a stark warning of the dangers that can dwell behind closed doors.

11

THE LAHORI PSYCHO

In December of 1999, a package arrived at a police office in Lahore, Pakistan. Inside, officers found a collection of photographs and a thirty-two-page diary. As they began to read, a story of unparalleled horror unfolded. The diary was a meticulous, detailed confession from a man who claimed to have raped and murdered exactly 100 boys over the course of the last eighteen months. A note included in the package provided an address, challenging the police to go there if they wanted proof. A quick check of the property records revealed the owner: a wealthy businessman named Javed Iqbal.

Javed Iqbal Mughal was born in Lahore in 1956, the 6th child in an affluent family. His father was a self-made man who worked himself to the point of exhaustion to ensure his children had every advantage. He worked punishing shifts, sometimes on as little as two hours of sleep, all to afford prestigious private schools, university fees, and trust funds for his children. Javed, like his siblings, grew up in a world of privilege, wanting for nothing. After graduating from university, he was given two large villas by his father. He chose to live in the larger one and, following his father's advice, set up a steel recasting business in the other.

As Javed entered his twenties, his parents began pressuring him to marry and start a family. He showed no interest. The pressure escalated to the point of threatening an arranged marriage, a prospect that caused Javed to break down completely. He begged for one last chance to find his own bride, even threatening to take his own life if they forced the issue. His parents relented.

Some months prior to this family drama, Javed had encountered a young homeless boy on the streets of Lahore. Moved by the child's plight, he took him into his home, clothing him and providing for him in what appeared to be an act of charity. When the pressure to marry became unbearable, Javed learned that this boy had an older sister who was also living on the streets. He asked the boy to introduce them. Ten minutes after meeting her, Javed decided this was the woman he would marry. For the young woman, who was homeless and destitute, marrying a wealthy man was a matter of survival. For Javed, it was a strategic move. By marrying the boy's sister, he was attempting to permanently bind the child to his life, making him family. The marriage was brief and produced one child before they separated. It was a union born of manipulation, not love, and it was doomed from the start.

Now single again and in his thirties, Javed's behavior grew more sinister. A family member visiting his home discovered that he was no longer housing just one boy; there were now six or seven young children living with the thirty-something-year-old man. The discovery was deeply unnerving, but it was soon overshadowed by a formal criminal accusation. Javed was charged with the rape and sodomy of one of the children living in his home.

The news of the crime ignited a firestorm of outrage in the community. A mob of townspeople, bent on revenge, descended on Javed's house. He wasn't there, but they found the other children he had been keeping. Frustrated, the mob moved on to his family's home, vandalizing it when they found it empty. Eventually, they tracked down Javed's father and brother at the family shop. The mob flooded into the store, beat both men, and then transported them to the police station in a rickshaw. It was there that the family was officially informed of the charges against Javed.

His father and brother were in denial, insisting Javed was not capable of such a thing. The police, however, claimed to have evidence. With Javed's whereabouts unknown, and uncertain of the family's involvement, the police took his father and brother into custody. Javed's father seemed more devastated by the damage to the family's reputation than by the suffering of his son's victim. His mother, however, was disgusted by her son's actions and resolved to help the police find him. She went to Javed's house and found a thirteen-year-old boy who claimed to have lived there for months. Believing it would lure her son out of hiding, she took the boy to the police station. The gambit worked. When Javed learned what his mother had done, he emerged to confront her, and the waiting police arrested him. For the rape and sodomy of a child, he was sentenced to just six months in jail.

While he was incarcerated, the stress of the situation caused Javed's father to suffer a serious heart attack. Though ashamed of the disgrace his son had brought upon the family, his father's loyalty never wavered. He spent a great deal of money trying to secure Javed's early release from prison. Upon his release, the family, aware of his predilections, pushed him into another marriage, hoping to steer him away from young boys. Like the first, this marriage was short-lived.

In 1992, Javed's father suffered another, fatal heart attack, an event precipitated by years of stress over his son's crimes. He was the last family member who maintained regular contact with Javed. With his father gone, the rest of the family, led by his disgusted mother, cut him off completely. From his father's estate, Javed inherited three million rupees (about 34,000 dollars). With this money, he purchased a large house in Lahore and set up a new business: a video game arcade. It was the first of its kind in the town, and it was strategically designed to attract his preferred victims. He would stand for hours, creepily watching the young boys who flocked to his establishment, singling out his favorites for free gifts and discount tokens.

He developed a particularly insidious tactic for luring his victims. He would slyly drop a 100-rupee note (about one dollar) on the floor, wait for a boy to pick it up, and then loudly announce that he had lost the money. When the boy who had taken the note remained silent, Javed would take him next door to his house and force him into a strip search, an act that frequently escalated into sexual assault.

This pattern of abuse continued for years. Shockingly, it was something of an open secret. The boys who frequented the arcade knew what the owner was like; they shared stories of his assaults among themselves, yet they kept coming back. Some parents and members of the community were also aware of what was happening behind the closed doors of the arcade, but nothing was ever done. Some of the parents who knew their children were being abused had been paid by Javed to keep silent. Others were too terrified of the notoriously corrupt Pakistani police to report the crimes, fearing that they could end up worse off for being seen as a nuisance.

In his mid-thirties, Javed's life took another dramatic turn when his arcade was robbed. He and an employee were beaten so severely they were nearly killed. The injuries left Javed bedridden for a long time, and he was forced to sell his house, his car, and what remained of his business to cover his hospital bills. During this period of convalescence, he was unable to care for his aging mother, who subsequently passed away. It is believed that this confluence of events — the violent assault, the loss of his wealth, and the death of his mother — was the catalyst that transformed Javed Iqbal from a serial child abuser into a serial killer.

Between 1998 and 1999, Javed began his killing spree. The streets of Lahore were home to as many as 5,000 homeless children, a vast and vulnerable population from which to choose his victims. He would lure them with the promise of food, shelter, and fresh clothing — the basic necessities they so desperately needed for survival. Once he had them in his home, he would photograph them, sometimes clothed, sometimes not, keeping a meticulous record of his crimes. He had set a goal for himself: he would kill exactly 100 boys and then he would stop. After sexually assaulting and strangling his victims, he would dismember their bodies and dissolve them in vats of acid.

When police, guided by the confessional diary, entered Javed's small, one-bedroom apartment, they found a house of horrors. Though the bodies were gone, the evidence was overwhelming. They collected fifty-eight pieces of children's clothing, along with the photographs he had taken of his victims. The news of the discovery sent shockwaves through the country. People were horrified that such atrocities could have been happening under their noses. The police put out a public announcement, asking parents of missing children to come to the station to try and identify the clothing. Hundreds of families came forward, revealing a hidden epidemic of missing children that had gone largely unreported due to the public's deep distrust of the police.

While the country reeled from the revelations, Javed Iqbal was nowhere to be found. The police launched one of the largest manhunts in Pakistan's history, focusing their search on the Ravi River, where Javed had mentioned in his diary he might go to drown himself. The manhunt came to a dramatic end on December 30, 1999. That morning, a disheveled-looking man burst into the offices of the Daily Jang newspaper. "I am Javed Iqbal, killer of a 100 boys," he announced to the stunned journalists. "I hate this world. I am not ashamed of my actions and I am ready to die. I have no regrets."

He had turned himself in to the media because he was convinced the police would kill him. The newspaper staff immediately called the authorities, and within minutes, the building was surrounded by 100 armed soldiers. Javed Iqbal was arrested, and later that evening, four fourteen-year-old boys — his accomplices — were taken into custody at his home. These boys, however, were not willing participants; they had been traumatized and forced to help him dismember the bodies of his victims. One of the boys would later die in police custody. The official cause of death was suicide — he had allegedly jumped from a high window — but it is widely believed that he was beaten to death by the police.

During his interrogation, Javed Iqbal was unrepentant. He said he could have killed 500 boys but stopped at 100 because that was his predetermined goal. His motives were twofold: a sick, sexual attraction to young boys, and a burning hatred for the police, whom he blamed for a brutal beating during a previous arrest that had left him crippled. In his diary, he wrote, "My mother cried for me. I want 100 mothers to cry for their children."

At his trial, Javed, along with his three surviving accomplices, changed his story completely. He denied everything, claiming the entire affair was an elaborate "social experiment" designed to raise awareness for the plight of runaway children. The court saw through his charade. He and his main accomplice were found guilty. The judge, in a move that reflected the public's outrage, delivered a shocking sentence: "You will be strangled to death in front of the parents whose children you killed. Your body will be cut into 100 pieces and put in acid, the same way you killed those children." The sentence was later revised to a standard execution after intervention from human rights officials.

In the aftermath, a strange and unsettling theory emerged, propagated by Javed's own brother. He claimed that Javed had been framed by the police, who needed a scapegoat to account for the hundreds of unsolved cases of missing boys in Lahore. He raised several compelling points. How could Javed have murdered and dismembered 100 boys in a small apartment with paper-thin walls without any of his neighbors hearing or seeing anything? Furthermore, how was it that several of the boys Javed had supposedly murdered had since turned up alive, reunited with their families?

On October 8, 2001, before any execution could be carried out, Javed Iqbal and his main accomplice were found dead in their prison cells. The official report stated that they had hanged themselves with their bedsheets in a suicide pact. An autopsy, however, told a different story. Both men had been savagely beaten just before their deaths. Javed's body was covered in injuries inflicted by a heavy, blunt weapon. In the end, it seemed, he had met the violent fate he feared at the hands of the very institution he so despised. None of his family members came to claim his body. A statement from the family declared, "We have nothing to do with him. He died for us on the day that he confessed to killing 100 children."

12

THE SUMMERFIELD SIX

The call to the authorities came after a confession, but not the kind made in the sterile confines of an interrogation room. This one was born of panic and guilt in a family home, when a news report about a missing teenager flashed across the television screen. At that moment, Kyle Hooper, a sixteen-year-old boy, broke down in front of his mother. He told her he knew what had happened to eighteen-year-old Seth Jackson, who had vanished the night of Sunday, April 17, 2011. The story he unburdened was so appalling that his mother immediately contacted the police. She pointed them toward a ramshackle house in Summerfield, Florida, indicating that this unassuming location was the site of a dark and gruesome secret.

When investigators arrived at the house, owned by eighteen-year-old Charlie Ely, they rounded up the young people present and began to unravel a story far more horrifying than they could have anticipated. One by one, they were brought to the station: Charlie Ely; Amber Wright, the fifteen-year-old ex-girlfriend of the missing boy; Kyle Hooper, Amber's half-brother; and Justin Soto, a twenty-year-old known to his friends as "Roach." All were residents or frequent guests at the house. The only person missing was another eighteen-year-old, Mike Bargo, a man who would soon be identified as the plot's central figure.

Seth Jackson was a typical teenager living in Summerfield with his parents, Scott and Sonia, and his two older brothers. He had a love for animals and harbored aspirations of one day competing in the Ultimate Fighting Championship, a dream his parents had agreed to support with training courses once he turned eighteen. He had been in a relationship with fifteen-year-old Amber Wright, and while it may have started happily, it soured after about a year. The situation was complicated further when Amber grew close to Mike Bargo, who was not just any rival but also Seth's best friend. The breakup, fueled by speculation that Amber had been cheating on him with Mike, left Seth traumatized.

On the night he disappeared, Sunday, April 17th, Seth was with his friend, Will Samalot. After visiting another friend, they began walking home shortly after 9:00 p.m. Will noticed that Seth seemed distracted, constantly texting on his phone. When the friends parted ways, it was the last time anyone other than his killers would see Seth Jackson alive. The next day, when he failed to return home, his mother, Sonia, filed a missing person's report.

The text messages recovered from Seth's phone told the story of his final hours. They were from Amber, who was proposing they meet to talk about "working things out." She told him she was bringing her friend Charlie Ely for support and instructed him where to wait. Seth's reply was laced with a chilling prescience. He warned her that if he got jumped, she could "say goodbye." Amber reassured him, claiming she could never do that and that she just wanted them to be back together. His last text message confirmed he was walking to their meeting spot, a corner where they had once fought.

At the sheriff's office, the interrogations began. Twenty-year-old Justin Soto was evasive from the start. He claimed to know nothing about a kid named Seth, other than that he was a "little white boy" who used to date Amber. When questioned about the fresh, deep scratches on his legs, he offered a flimsy excuse about walking through the woods and getting tangled in vines. The detectives were not convinced. The scratches looked more like the result of running through the dark woods, not a casual walk. His answers were vague, and he repeatedly used phrases like "pretty much," a verbal tic that often signals a person is withholding the full truth.

In separate rooms, Amber Wright and Charlie Ely presented a coordinated version of events. They admitted that Amber had lured Seth to the house under the pretense of a reconciliation. They claimed that after they talked for a while, Seth showed up at Charlie's house unannounced about an hour later. According to their initial story, Seth was sitting in a chair when, without any warning, Kyle Hooper emerged and struck him. In this telling, they were innocent bystanders who, frightened by the sudden violence, fled to a bedroom and hid. They said they heard Mike Bargo's door fly open, followed by a series of gunshots. They claimed they remained in the room until the next morning, emerging to a house that smelled strongly of bleach. They both insisted that Justin Soto was not even there that night.

The entire narrative constructed by Justin, Amber, and Charlie collapsed when detectives confronted them with the confession of Kyle Hooper. After being separated from his mother, the sixteen-year-old finally unburdened himself of the complete, horrific truth. His story began not with the murder, but with the turmoil in his own life. He explained that he had been fighting with his parents and, feeling alienated, had moved into Charlie's house. His anger and frustration were simmering on the night of the murder.

Kyle told detectives that the group, including Justin Soto, was at the house when Mike Bargo, high on an unknown quantity of white pills he had been snorting, became agitated and violent. When Seth's name came up, Mike declared his intention to kill him that night and asked the others if they were "down." The motive was a potent mix of jealousy and wounded pride. Mike was with Amber, but the animosity with Seth ran deeper. The two had recently gotten into a physical fight, which Seth had apparently won, deeply humiliating Mike.

Kyle admitted that he, too, hated Seth, claiming he had found Seth in bed with his ex-girlfriend. But the driving force, he insisted, was Mike. He recounted how Mike had volunteered to take all the blame, assuring the others he had nothing to lose. With that assurance, the plan was solidified. Kyle stated unequivocally that everyone present agreed to the murder: Amber, Charlie, Justin Soto, himself, and Mike Bargo. Amber's role was to be the bait. She was to call Seth and lure him to the house.

Faced with Kyle's detailed confession, the other stories crumbled. The detectives now had the leverage they needed. One by one, they confronted Justin, Amber, and Charlie with the truth, pointing out the inconsistencies in their fabricated tales. The pressure mounted until each of them broke. Charlie was the first of the girls to admit she knew something violent was planned. Amber, confronted with her brother's account, finally confessed her role in knowingly luring Seth to his death. Justin, told that everyone else was blaming him, abandoned his pretense of ignorance and began to recount his part in the events of that night.

With the confessions aligned, a single, horrifying narrative of Seth Jackson's murder emerged. When Seth arrived at the house, he was led into a trap. As he sat in a chair, Kyle Hooper approached from behind and struck him over the head with a wooden stick, hitting him so hard the stick broke into pieces. Justin Soto then joined the assault, also hitting Seth with a stick. Wounded, Seth tried to flee toward the kitchen, but Mike Bargo appeared and shot him in the back with a .22 caliber revolver.

As Seth fell, Justin grabbed him in a chokehold while Mike continued to shoot him, firing approximately five rounds into his body. Kyle recounted the harrowing moments that followed, describing how he was ordered to drag Seth's body, which was still partially alive, up the stairs and into a bathroom. Inside the bathroom, the brutality escalated. With Seth lying in the bathtub, Mike continued his frenzied attack, punching him repeatedly. Kyle described having to physically pull Mike away from the body. It was then, with Seth either dying or already dead, that Mike began to break his kneecaps with a hard object, a final act of desecration.

After the murder, the group's focus shifted to disposing of the evidence. They wrapped Seth's body in a blue sleeping bag and carried it out to a fire pit in the backyard. Justin admitted it was his job to tend the fire, for which he had been collecting firewood. To mask the smell of the burning body, they threw two old car tires onto the pyre. As the body burned through the night, Mike Bargo continued to display a depraved and psychopathic demeanor. Kyle described how, even after Seth was dead, Mike struck the body with a shovel as it lay in the fire pit.

The following morning, the grizzly task continued. Kyle recalled watching Mike sift through the ashes in the fire pit, picking out teeth and fragments of Seth's skull and casually playing with the victim's tongue before placing the remains into paint containers. The final step of the disposal involved Amber and Kyle's stepfather, James Havens III. According to multiple accounts, Amber texted Havens and asked him to come to the house. Once there, Havens helped Mike and Justin load the paint cans filled with Seth's remains, along with cinder blocks, into the back of his truck. Mike directed them to a remote, water-filled quarry, a place he knew from a past swimming trip. There, they tied the cinder blocks to the buckets with a dog leash and threw them into the water, hoping to conceal their crime forever.

While the four suspects were confessing at the station, Mike Bargo was still at large. He had fled to the town of Starke, Florida, seeking refuge at the home of his new girlfriend's father, James Williams Sr. Unaware of the true reason for his visit, Williams offered him a place to stay. However, Mike's conscience, or perhaps his ego, wouldn't allow him to stay silent. He confessed to Williams, fabricating a story that he had killed a man who had assaulted his sister. He then told Williams's girlfriend, Crystal Anderson, the entire story of Seth's murder, claiming he had done it because Seth had allegedly assaulted Amber. After Williams convinced him to surrender, the police, who had already tracked him to the location, surrounded the house and took him into custody. Brought to an interrogation room, Mike Bargo was read his rights. Before any meaningful questioning could begin, he invoked his right to an attorney, and the interview was promptly terminated.

The so-called "Summerfield Six" — Mike Bargo, Amber Wright, Kyle Hooper, Charlie Ely, Justin Soto, and James Havens III — were all charged for their roles in the murder of Seth Jackson. James Havens III pleaded guilty to being an accessory after the fact for his role in disposing of the body. The others went to trial. Amber Wright, Kyle Hooper, and Justin Soto were all convicted of first-degree murder and sentenced to life in prison. Charlie Ely was also convicted of first-degree murder and received a life sentence, but in 2020, after serving nearly a decade, she was granted a retrial. She accepted a plea deal for second-degree murder and was freed at the age of 27.

As the mastermind and triggerman, Mike Bargo faced the stiffest penalty. He was convicted of first-degree murder and sentenced to death. He currently awaits his fate on Florida's death row. As he was led from the courtroom after his sentencing, his final reported words were, "May God have mercy on my soul."

13

THE PRINCE OF FRAUD

After purchasing two Rolex watches, a gold bracelet, and a massive diamond pinky ring, the man known as Prince Khalid of Saudi Arabia boarded a private jet bound for New York. Upon landing, his limousine delivered him to the Four Seasons Hotel, where he had rented out the entire top floor. As he settled in to enjoy a meal from room service, a loud, insistent knock shattered the opulent tranquility. Before he could react, two men burst through the door. They beat him, forced him into a car, and drove him back to the airport. During a moment of inattention, the prince managed to slip away, frantically alerting police that he had been kidnapped by two armed men.

However, when officers arrived, they did not arrest the alleged kidnappers. Instead, the man they put in handcuffs was the prince himself. It turned out that he was not Prince Khalid, nor was he even Arab. He was a con man from Michigan named Anthony Gignac, and for the better part of 30 years, he had been successfully posing as a member of the Saudi royal family, swindling millions of dollars from his victims. The two men who had taken him were not kidnappers but bounty hunters, tasked with returning him to Miami to face justice for his long list of crimes.

The story of Anthony Gignac began in 1970, far from the gilded palaces he would one day claim as his own. He was born, not Anthony Gignac, but Jose Moreno in the slums of Bogota, Colombia. According to Gignac's own account — a narrative that requires a healthy dose of skepticism — his early life was a relentless trauma. He claimed that he and his brother, Daniel, ran away from home after their father murdered their younger brother, unable to afford to feed all three children. For the next two years, the boys lived on the streets, with Jose resorting to selling his body just to ensure his brother had food. All of this, he alleged, happened before he was six years old.

After two years on the streets, the Moreno brothers were adopted by Nancy and Jim Gignac and brought to the suburbs of Michigan, where Jose was renamed Anthony. Life in America was an improvement, but it was not easy. Anthony was bullied at school for his appearance and had few friends. He found his escape in television, specifically in a show called *Lifestyles of the Rich and Famous*, which ignited a lifelong obsession with wealth, power, and fame that would ultimately consume him.

His career as a grifter began in the 6th grade. His adopted mother received a call from a local car dealership, informing her that the "prince's" Mercedes was ready for pickup. twelve-year-old Tony had convinced the dealership that he was a Saudi prince and that his father, the king, would settle the bill later. They had even allowed him to test drive the vehicle. This incident convinced his parents that he had serious mental health issues, and he spent much of his adolescence in mental institutions. At seventeen, he ran away from home for good. He soon found lodging with an Arab family by threatening them, claiming to be Saudi royalty and warning that his father's secret police would come after them if they refused him shelter. His stay was brief, however, as he was soon arrested for impersonating Adnan Khashoggi, a Saudi arms dealer who was, at the time, the richest man in the world.

After this arrest, Gignac fled Michigan for California, believing that if he could deceive actual Arab people, scamming others would be even easier. He was correct. For the next several years, he perfected his craft, grifting his way across the United States. He wore designer clothes, rode in limousines, and dined on fine food, living out the fantasy he had seen on television. His method was simple and repeatable: he would convince people he was a Saudi prince, they would provide him with free goods and services, and eventually, when the scheme was discovered, he would go to jail. Upon release, he would simply move to a new city and begin the cycle anew.

His exploits earned him the nickname "The Prince of Fraud." In 1991, while posing as Prince Khalid Al-Saud, he ran up a $10,000 bill on limousines and luxury hotels and conned Rodeo Drive shopkeepers out of Louis Vuitton luggage and a rare coin collection. After that four-day spree, he was arrested. From there, he went to San Francisco, where he stayed at the Ritz-Carlton for two months under the prince's name before being sent back to prison. His most audacious early scam occurred in 1993, when he checked into a premier Hawaiian resort and racked up a $20,000 bill, which he managed to pay off by selling an imaginary oil field to another hotel guest. This pattern of audacious fraud and subsequent arrest continued for years until a scam in Chicago involving $50,000 worth of clothing from Saks Fifth Avenue landed him in more serious trouble.

Facing his 27th offense, Gignac knew he needed a top-tier lawyer. He even managed to get a meeting with Johnnie Cochran, of O.J. Simpson trial fame, but Cochran refused the case due to "questions about authenticity." Gignac then found a lawyer named Oscar Rodriguez, whom he success-fully convinced that he was, in fact, the prince. He promised Rodriguez that if he took the case, he would be made the personal attorney for the entire Saudi royal family in the United States. Though skeptical, Rodriguez was swayed by the small chance that the story was true and posted Gignac's $50,000 bail, with the understanding that the royal family would reimburse him within twenty-four hours.

When the money never arrived, Rodriguez had to return his client to jail. It was then that Gignac hatched another brilliant idea. He told Rodriguez to take him to an American Express office. Thirty minutes later, in an era of less stringent financial security, Gignac walked out with a credit card that had a $200 million line of credit. He immediately paid Rodriguez back and embarked on one of the most unhinged shopping sprees in history, buying Rolexes, jewelry, and fine art. Any doubts Rodriguez had were erased, until a frantic call from American Express confirmed that Gignac was a fraud and that he needed to be stopped before he spent the entire $200 million. By then, Gignac was already on a plane to New York. Panicked, Rodriguez sent two bounty hunters to capture him, which led to the chaotic scene at the Four Seasons and LaGuardia Airport.

The genius behind Gignac's long-running scam was revealed during the legal proceedings. He had been able to gain access to accounts and secure lines of credit because he had legally changed his name to Khalid bin Al-Saud. His Social Security number, immigration records, and college transcripts were all under that name. On paper, he was the prince, and he had the documents to prove it. Despite this cleverness, he was sentenced to four years in prison, with another three added after a failed escape attempt involving a fire and shampoo-covered floors.

Upon his next release, Gignac decided he needed to be a "better criminal." He was tired of short-lived scams and wanted to enjoy the princely lifestyle for longer stretches. He recognized his weakness was on the business side of his cons, so he sought a partner who could provide legitimacy and business acumen. He found that partner in Carl Williamson, a London-born banker with extensive connections to the wealthy. Together, they launched a new venture called Martin Williamson International.

Their primary scheme revolved around the highly anticipated initial public offering (IPO) of Saudi Aramco, the sixth largest company in the world. Williamson, claiming to have known Gignac for twenty years, told potential investors they could get in on the IPO before it went public. He showed them fraudulent documents proving Gignac had over $2 billion in assets. The pitch worked, and they collected $8 million from twenty-six different investors.

For Gignac, however, it was never just about the money; it was about the image. He flaunted his wealth on Instagram with a constant stream of posts featuring luxury cars, piles of cash, and Rolexes. His dog even wore a diamond collar. This social media presence wasn't just for show; it added a layer of credibility to his persona. Between photos of his lavish lifestyle, he would post pictures of actual Saudi royals, which he claimed to have taken himself.

Their success with the IPO scheme emboldened them, and they set their sights on a much larger target: billionaire real estate heir Jeff Soffer, whose family owned the famed Fontainebleau Hotel in Miami. The hotel had been in debt for years, so Soffer was receptive when a supposed Saudi prince called with a massive investment offer. Gignac and Soffer began spending time together, even flying on a private plane to Aspen to discuss business.

This trip, however, marked the beginning of the end for the Prince of Fraud. Soffer had been secretly running a background check on Gignac. When Gignac got word of this, he feigned outrage and threatened to call off the deal. A panicked Soffer, on the advice of Carl Williamson, gave Gignac a lavish Cartier bracelet as a peace offering. The gesture seemed to work, and to smooth things over, Soffer invited Gignac to a fancy dinner. It was there that Gignac made his fatal mistake: he ordered an appetizer containing prosciutto, a pork product forbidden in Islam.

The detail clicked in Soffer's mind. He started reviewing Gignac's Instagram feed through a new lens, noticing all the other non-Islamic behaviors: his ownership of dogs, his consumption of alcohol, his gambling — all proudly advertised to the world. While true Arab royals might indulge in such activities privately, they would never be so brazenly public about them. Soffer knew he had been duped. He had his private investigator confirm his suspicions, which took only five minutes, and then alerted the State Department and the Federal Bureau of Investigation (FBI).

By then, Gignac was traveling the world, living lavishly off his ill-gotten gains. While he was away, federal agents built their case, raiding his Miami penthouse and seizing half a million dollars' worth of jewelry, cash, and art. When Gignac finally returned to the United States, federal agents swarmed him before he could even get off the plane, swapping his diamond bracelets for a pair made of stainless steel. He was charged with wire fraud, conspiracy, and aggravated identity theft. His partner, Carl Williamson, was also charged as a co-conspirator. Facing the prospect of a long prison sentence, Williamson hanged himself in his home.

Anthony Gignac was found guilty on all charges and sentenced to eighteen years in federal prison. In a twisted way, after a lifetime of deception, he finally achieved the one thing he had always craved above all else: he might not have the riches, but he was finally, undeniably famous.

14

THE CELEBRITY CANNIBAL

In the summer of 1981, a small man living in a quiet apartment in the Latin Quarter of Paris prepared for dinner. His name was Issei Sagawa, a Japanese doctoral student in comparative literature at the Sorbonne. He was unassuming in appearance—thin, frail, and barely over five feet (about 152 centimeters) tall. To his neighbors, he was polite and soft-spoken, the kind of man who seemed perpetually lost in his books. But that evening, he was waiting for a woman named Renée Hartevelt, a fellow student he admired deeply. She had agreed to come by and help him with a German poem he wanted to record for study. When she arrived, she had no reason to suspect that the man she considered a harmless friend had spent years imagining the moment he might kill and eat another human being.

Issei Sagawa was born on April 26, 1949, in Kobe, Japan. He came from wealth and privilege. His father was a powerful businessman — president of Kurita Water Industries—while his grandfather had been the editor of one of Japan's largest newspapers. His mother stayed home to care for the family, and by all accounts, the Sagawa household was loving, traditional, and financially secure. There was no history of neglect or violence, no trauma that might foreshadow the horrors their eldest son would later commit. Yet, from the moment he entered the world, something about Issei seemed offbeat, fragile, and uncertain.

He was born prematurely, so small that his father could hold him in the palm of one hand. As a baby, he suffered from enteritis, an inflammation of the intestines that nearly killed him. The doctors' treatments saved his life but left him sickly and frail. Throughout childhood, his delicate health kept him apart from other children. He was quiet, shy, and often lost in his imagination. Books became his refuge. He read constantly — fairy tales, folklore, and literature that transported him away from the weak, awkward body he despised. In the stories he loved, heroes triumphed over monsters. Yet somewhere in his mind, those monsters began to fascinate him more than the heroes did.

He later described a memory from his early years, a moment that stayed with him for life. His uncle had once played a game with him and his younger brother, pretending to be a man-eating giant who chased them around the house. Their father would "rescue" them in the end, and everyone would laugh. For most children, it was harmless fun, but Issei recalled an emotion he didn't understand — a strange mix of fear and excitement, something deeper than play. He would later say that this was his first awakening, the moment he became fascinated by stories of cannibalism. Tales like *Hansel and Gretel* — where children are nearly eaten by a witch — stirred something in him. They frightened him, but they also thrilled him. He didn't know why.

The Sagawa household was affectionate but reserved. Sex was a topic no one ever mentioned. As a result, when Issei reached adolescence and his body began to change, he didn't understand what was happening. The first time he experienced sexual arousal, he thought he was ill. Without any guidance or discussion, his curiosity took dark turns. He began to act out secret experiments — things that left him ashamed but also confusedly exhilarated. His understanding of desire became warped, tangled up with guilt and secrecy. By the time he was a teenager, his fantasies had already begun to merge with violence.

When he was around six years old, he experienced another memory that haunted him. He looked at the bare thighs of a classmate and thought to himself that he wanted to bite them. He was just a child, but the thought felt instinctive. As he grew older, the urge didn't fade. Instead, it became more specific: he imagined consuming women — especially those he found beautiful, strong, and healthy, everything he believed he was not.

By the time he reached high school, Issei understood that these thoughts were not normal. At fifteen, he tried to seek psychiatric help, contacting a psychologist, but he never went through with it. He couldn't bring himself to confess such fantasies to anyone, especially his parents. From the outside, he remained the quiet, bookish son of a respectable family, but internally, his mind was already turning toward something monstrous.

After earning his master's degree in English literature in Japan, Sagawa enrolled at Wako University in Tokyo. He was intelligent and deeply interested in Western culture, particularly European literature. Yet even as he read the classics, his dark fascination persisted. In 1972, when he was 24, he saw a tall, blonde German woman walking along a Tokyo street. To most men, she might have been simply beautiful. To Issei, she was prey. That summer, he followed her home. Late one night, he crept through her unlocked window, clutching an umbrella as a makeshift weapon. She was asleep and naked. He later claimed that he didn't intend to kill her — he just wanted to take a bite of her flesh. Before he could act, she woke, screamed, and overpowered him easily.

The police arrived quickly and arrested him, charging him with attempted rape. The true intention behind his intrusion was never revealed to authorities. His wealthy father intervened, paid a settlement to the victim, and ensured that the charges were dropped. Issei walked free. Nothing in his life changed, except that his fantasies grew more powerful. He had come close to realizing them, and now he knew they were not impossible.

Nine years later, in 1981, Issei Sagawa was living in Paris. He had moved there to pursue a PhD in comparative literature at the Sorbonne, one of Europe's most prestigious universities. His new life seemed cosmopolitan, even romantic — a young Japanese scholar in the heart of France, surrounded by art and intellectuals. But inside his small apartment in the city's Latin Quarter, he lived a double life. By day he attended lectures and read poetry; by night he visited sex workers, bringing them back to his apartment with a gun hidden in his bag. He never followed through, always freezing at the last moment. But every attempt brought him closer to the reality of what he wanted to do.

It was during this time that he met Renée Hartevelt. She was 25, Dutch, and brilliant. A fellow PhD student studying French literature, she was tall, elegant, and fluent in three languages. To Issei, she embodied everything he admired and envied. He saw in her a kind of perfection — intellectual, physical, and moral. They met in class, and he quickly found a way to spend time with her. Claiming that he needed help improving his German, he offered to pay her for tutoring sessions, supported, he said, by his father's wealth. Renée agreed. She considered him an odd but kind friend, someone who seemed lonely and harmless.

Over the following weeks, they met regularly. They talked about literature, music, and art. Renée enjoyed his company but to Issei, these meetings became unbearable. He wanted more than friendship. He wanted to consume her — to literally take her into himself. In his own words, he felt small, weak, and ugly, while she was tall and beautiful. He believed that by eating her, he could somehow absorb her vitality. It was a delusion, but one that had obsessed him for decades.

One evening, he invited her to his apartment for dinner, asking her to read aloud from a German poem he admired. She sat at his desk, her back to him, unaware that a rifle was hidden in a drawer nearby. He raised the gun to shoot, but it jammed. She didn't notice. He laughed nervously, pretended nothing had happened, and saw her off as though the night had been ordinary. But the failure only deepened his obsession.

A few days later, on June 11, 1981, he invited her again under the same pretext. This time, he offered her tea, secretly mixed with whiskey. When she seemed relaxed, he confessed that he loved her. Renée, polite but firm, told him she valued his friendship but did not feel the same way. She tried to let him down gently and Issei said he understood. Then he handed her the book of poems and asked her to read. She sat down, facing the window, and began. Behind her, he raised the rifle. The shot entered her neck. For a moment, she kept reading before collapsing to the floor.

The sound of the gun had been muffled by the apartment's thick walls. No one came. Issei fainted briefly, overcome by shock. When he woke, the reality of what he had done began to settle. He had killed her. And now, his fantasy could finally be realized.

He laid a towel beneath her head, undressed her, and began to prepare her body. His obsession had always focused on one part of the body—the thighs and buttocks. He attempted to bite into the flesh but found his teeth too weak. He fetched a fruit knife, then a sharper one, but neither worked. Finally, he left the apartment and went to a store, purchasing a meat knife. With it, he began cutting. Later, he described the taste and texture in grotesque detail, comparing the fat to corn-colored butter and the flesh to raw tuna. He cooked some portions, ate others raw, experimenting with sauces and seasonings. He took photographs of each stage, documenting the process as if it were a ritual or a study.

For two days, he continued, storing pieces of her in plastic bags and the refrigerator. When the body began to decay and flies appeared, he realized he had to dispose of it. He dismembered the remains, placed them in two large suitcases, and called a taxi. The driver helped him load the heavy bags and joked, "What's in here, a body?" Issei smiled weakly and said they were full of books.

He asked to be taken to the Bois de Boulogne, a large park west of Paris. It was evening, around eight p.m., and the park was still busy. As he struggled to drag the suitcases toward a secluded lake, passersby watched him curiously. The small man sweating and dragging two bulky cases drew attention. Feeling overwhelmed, he left the bags near the water's edge and walked a few steps away to catch his breath. At that moment, an older man nearby called out, asking if the bags were his. Issei replied that they were not and walked away quickly.

The man, suspicious, opened one of the cases. Inside, wrapped in a blood-soaked sheet, was a human torso. He screamed for help. Police arrived within minutes, cordoned off the area, and began their investigation. Witnesses described a small Japanese man as the one who had left the suitcases. It did not take long for detectives to connect him to the address of a local student — Issei Sagawa.

When police entered his apartment, they found the evidence unmistakable. The refrigerator contained human remains. Photographs, tools, and books lay scattered around the room. Issei did not resist. When asked why he had done it, he replied calmly that he had killed her to eat her flesh.

Despite the confession and overwhelming evidence, the legal process that followed was a failure of justice. The French court deemed him mentally unfit to stand trial, diagnosing him as legally insane. He was sent to a psychiatric institution rather than prison, where he remained for only two years. His father hired prominent lawyers and paid for his care. In 1984, after negotiations between France and Japan, he was deported to his home country, officially transferred to a hospital in Tokyo.

Upon arrival, Japanese doctors examined him and declared him sane— but evil. They believed his crime had been driven not by psychosis but by perversion and desire. Yet because the French authorities refused to release the case documents, Japan had no legal evidence to prosecute him. Without those files, there could be no trial. After fifteen months of obser- vation, the hospital released him on August 12, 1986. He walked out a free man.

The reaction in Japan was unlike anything the French could have imag- ined. Instead of disgust or fear, the media treated Issei Sagawa as a morbid celebrity. His crime became a national curiosity. Newspapers published interviews, magazines offered him columns, and publishers commissioned books. He wrote essays describing the murder in chilling detail, later collected in a best-selling volume that sold over 200,000 copies. Photographs from the crime scene — leaked illegally — circulated in print, turning the tragedy of Renée Hartevelt into spectacle.

Sagawa became a frequent guest on talk shows, where he spoke openly about cannibalism. He drew cartoons and wrote novels that mixed fantasy and confession. He acted in low-budget films and even appeared in pornography, often cast as himself — a man whose notoriety was his only appeal. In one adult film, he lived for a day with a co-star, and after they had sex, he revealed who he was, showing her photographs of his crime. The woman burst into tears. Yet, strangely, they remained friends afterward.

For years, Sagawa lived off the income from these appearances and from royalties. He published a comic book featuring graphic illustrations of the murder. He painted nude women, selling the artworks to collectors. He was both reviled and fascinated by the attention, calling himself cursed by his own freedom. "Not being able to live as a normal person," he told *Vice* in 2009, "is my punishment." But his statements lacked remorse. In that same interview, he admitted that his desires had never disappeared. Even as an aging man, he said, he still fantasized about consuming human flesh. On his way to the interview, he confessed, he had seen a woman on the street and imagined eating her legs.

By that point, his life had deteriorated into quiet decay. He lived alone in a small apartment outside Tokyo, supported occasionally by his younger brother. In 2013, he suffered a cerebral hemorrhage that left him paralyzed and confined to a wheelchair. He could no longer eat solid food and was fed through a tube. Yet even then, he spoke publicly about his wish to die at the hands of a beautiful woman, slowly and painfully, as if to complete some twisted cycle of desire and death.

Renée Hartevelt's family never spoke publicly about her murder. They avoided interviews, refusing to turn their daughter's tragedy into spectacle. Their silence stands in stark contrast to the noise that surrounded her killer. For them, there was only grief and disbelief: a young woman full of promise, her life taken and desecrated, while the man who killed her became infamous and free.

Issei Sagawa's story is one of failure — not just personal but systemic. The legal loopholes that allowed his release exposed the fragility of justice when nations fail to cooperate. His transformation from murderer to media figure revealed society's own morbid fascination with evil. Over time, his fame faded, but he never expressed true guilt. Instead, he lived out his remaining years as a symbol of horror — an aging man trapped inside a body that once longed to consume others, reduced now to one that could barely feed itself.

15

THE HOLY ROLLERS CULT

In 1903, the small farming community of Corvallis, Oregon, was the epitome of a town where time moved at a slower, more predictable pace. It was a place where everyone knew everyone else's business, where secrets were impossible to keep, and where the local newspaper reported on the mundane triumphs of its citizens, such as a man's swift bicycle journey to a neighboring town or the comical terror of a store employee who mistook a large rat for a panther. Life was simple, quiet, and largely uneventful. That all changed the day a stranger strolled into town with a fierce knowledge of scripture, a disarming charm, and a bold, world-altering declaration: he had a direct line to God. The man's name was Franz Edmund Creffield, and his arrival would unleash a torrent of religious fanaticism that would rapidly devolve into a bizarre and dangerous cult, plunging the once-peaceful community into a constant state of chaos filled with rumors of strange rituals, orgies, and ultimately, a string of violent deaths that would leave families shattered for decades to come.

Little is known about Franz Creffield's life before he appeared in Oregon. It is believed he was born in Germany sometime in the 1870s, and based on his later obsession with scripture, it's thought he came from a deeply religious background, perhaps even having formally studied theology. By the time he was in his twenties, he had made his way to the United States, and records place him as a member of the Salvation Army, Protestant Christian church and an international charitable organisation, in Oregon by 1899. For a time, the organization, with its military-style ranks and focus on evangelical charity work, seemed a perfect fit for the intensely devout young man. He excelled, and the higher-ups, seeing his potential as a future leader, even selected him for officer training school.

But something inside Creffield began to shift. He grew even more fanatical in his beliefs, and a rift formed between him and the other members. He started to openly criticize the Salvation Army's focus on fundraising, believing they were placing too much emphasis on money and not enough on pure spirituality. The conflict festered until, in 1901, Creffield claimed to have been visited by the Holy Spirit, who delivered a divine message: the Salvation Army was not entirely of God, and he was to leave its ranks immediately. He obeyed, traveling to Salem, Oregon, where he enrolled in a training school for aspiring preachers run by a Pentecostal minister named Martin L. Ryan.

For a while, he seemed to thrive under Ryan's teachings, but soon, the Holy Spirit allegedly appeared to him again, this time with a far grander pronouncement. The spirit told Creffield that he was God's chosen one. This anointing filled him with a new sense of purpose and arrogance. Believing he no longer needed anyone's guidance, he decided he was ready to set out on his own and establish a new church with himself as its one true prophet. In 1903, he left Salem and traveled forty miles (about sixty-five kilometers) south, arriving in the unsuspecting town of Corvallis.

Creffield knew that if he simply walked into town and announced his divine status, he would be dismissed as a lunatic. He had to ease people into his radical theology, so he began by preaching conventional sermons about being a good person and helping one's neighbors, singing familiar hymns, and hosting services that felt no different from any other church in the area. This approach allowed him to slowly build a small but loyal following. Once he had gained their trust, he began to subtly introduce his own unique doctrines. He spoke of how God had communicated with him directly, and he promised his followers that if they gave themselves over to God completely, they too could one day hear His voice. He introduced the concept of a "holy roll" in heaven, a sacred list upon which their names could be written, guaranteeing their salvation. But, he also said space on this roll was limited, forcing them to commit to his teachings fully and immediately or risk eternal damnation.

This tactic worked. While some were skeptical and left his services, a significant number of people, many of them disillusioned former members of the Salvation Army, were captivated by his message and became his most devoted followers. With his core group secured, Creffield began to introduce stranger and more intense practices. He focused heavily on hell and repentance, and he instilled in his flock a sense of superiority, claiming that because they were led by a true prophet, they were inherently better than all other religious groups. He also claimed to possess divine healing powers, waving his hands over his followers and praying until they believed they had been cured of their ailments.

The centerpiece of his new church was the ritual of repentance. These sessions were anything but peaceful. Creffield would have his followers pray over each other for hours on end, their prayers escalating into convulsive screams and chants. He then instructed them to roll around on the ground, praying to heaven, sometimes for as long as twenty-four hours straight. The effect of this practice was profound. Mentally and physically exhausted, sleep-deprived, and disoriented from the endless rolling, his followers would begin to experience auditory and visual hallucinations, which they interpreted as the divine messages Creffield had promised. This shared delusion sealed their faith. They were utterly convinced that Creffield was a true prophet who had given them the secret to communicating directly with God.

These loud and chaotic meetings quickly drew the ire of the other townspeople. The all-night screaming and chanting made sleep impossible, and the behavior of Creffield's female followers became a source of local scandal. The constant rolling left their hair undone and disheveled, and they often walked around barefoot, actions considered immodest for women of that era. Words like "sect" and "cult" began to circulate, and the townspeople mockingly dubbed the group the "Holy Rollers" for their bizarre rituals. After months of escalating tension, the community had had enough and city officials formally banned Creffield from holding his services within the Corvallis city limits. The town hoped this would be the end of the matter, but for Creffield's followers, their faith was unshakable.

Creffield, ever the opportunist, claimed that God had once again visited him, conveniently instructing him to move his flock to Smith Island, a small, uninhabited piece of land just three miles (about five kilometers) outside of town. In the summer of 1903, approximately twenty of his most loyal followers abandoned their jobs, their homes, and in some cases, their spouses and children, to join him.

Among those who followed him to the island were several key figures whose lives would become tragically intertwined with the cult's fate. There was the Hurt family, led by the patriarch O.V. Hurt and his wife, Sarah. Their twenty-three-year-old daughter, Maud, a woman described as both beautiful and intensely intelligent, had been a religious prodigy since childhood and became one of Creffield's most ardent disciples. She convinced her mother, Sarah, her sister May, and her brother Frank to join her on the island, terrified that their souls would be lost if they didn't get their names on the holy roll. Frank's fiancée, Molly Sandell, also joined the exodus. Then there were Donna and Esther Mitchell, two sisters from a family of seven children who had been abandoned by their father after their mother's death. Donna was married to a man named Burgess Starr, while fifteen-year-old Esther had left the Salvation Army to follow Creffield. The group also included Cora Hartley and her daughter Sophie, the wife and child of Lewis Hartley, by far the wealthiest man in the region, who despised Creffield and the hold he had on his family.

On Smith Island, away from the prying eyes of society, Creffield's control intensified. They lived in tents and spent their days in a state of constant religious frenzy, with multi-day "roll-a-thons" becoming a regular occurrence. Creffield's talk of the apocalypse ramped up, and he proclaimed himself "Joshua the Holy Prophet," a name his followers dutifully adopted. He ordered them to shed their worldly possessions, forcing them to wear thin, simple dresses or sometimes nothing at all.

The first sign of his manipulative nature came when he targeted Maud Hurt's wealthy fiancé, James Barry, who had provided the seed money for

Creffield's church. When Creffield demanded Barry fund the construction of a tabernacle, Barry not only refused but asked when Creffield planned to repay the initial loan. Enraged, Creffield claimed God had canceled the debt and ordered a stunned Maud to immediately break off their engagement, which she did without hesitation. After this, he systematically broke up all the other unmarried couples in the group.

He then implemented a deeply disturbing ceremony he called being "endowed with the grace of love." He would summon the women and girls of the cult, one by one, into his private tent for hours of supposed "prayer." While what happened inside was never definitively proven, it's widely believed he manipulated them into performing sexual acts under the guise of religious purification. At the end of each session, he would order the woman, regardless of her age or marital status, to kiss him. Any refusal was met with accusations of demonic possession, followed by brutal beatings to "drive the devil out." When some of the men in the group began to express doubts about his methods, Creffield swiftly kicked them out, consolidating his power and leaving himself with a flock of mostly compliant women. One of the men kicked out, Burgess Starr, later told reporters that Creffield had his followers so completely in his power that they would have jumped into a river if he had commanded it.

At the end of the summer, with the weather turning cold, the group needed a new place to stay. Maud Hurt offered up her family's home, which was conveniently located just outside the Corvallis city limits where Creffield's ban was not in effect. Her father, O.V. Hurt had been waiting all summer for his family to return, and though he despised Creffield, he tolerated the cult's presence in his home just to be reunited with his wife and children. His reward for this devotion was constant torment. The cult members, including his own family, refused to call him by his name, referring to him only as the "black devil" and constantly warning him that God would smite him for his lack of faith. After months of this psychological abuse, the beleaguered O.V. Hurt finally broke and joined the group himself.

With the entire Hurt family now under his control, Creffield's behavior grew even more erratic. During a traditional spring cleaning, he ordered his followers not to clean the house, but to burn it. They dragged all of the Hurt family's possessions outside and threw them onto a giant bonfire, along with items brought from their own former homes in Corvallis. They also sacrificed a dog, and rumors began to swirl that they had sacrificed Hurt's adopted toddler, Martha, as well. The rumor, though false, prompted a police visit. The officers who entered the Hurt home walked into a scene of pure madness. The cult members were scattered around a room in a trance-like state, some kneeling, some rolling on the floor, all looking pale and haggard with hollowed eyes. In the center of the room, a young girl with a cloth over her head was channeling a message from God while others wrote down her words.

The visit from the police did little to slow Creffield's descent. After O.V. was briefly convinced to leave the cult and kicked the group out of his house, they moved into the nearby home of Frank and Molly Hurt. It was there that Creffield had his most audacious revelation yet: God had commanded him to find a woman who would become the next Virgin Mary and bear the second Christ. He claimed he could "purify" the women of their past sins, making even mothers eligible for this holy duty. This was the origin of the group's other name, the "Brides of Christ," and it served as Creffield's justification for having sex with all the women and underage girls in the cult, often in group orgies, under the pretext of purification. He first chose sixteen-year-old Esther Mitchell to be his bride, but her older sister had her committed to an orphanage to protect her. His next choice was Maud Hurt.

But before he could marry Maud, a vigilante group of twenty local men calling themselves the "White Caps" stormed the house in the middle of the night. They kidnapped Creffield and the other male members, marched them naked through the center of Corvallis, and publicly tarred and feathered them as a warning to leave town for good. Undeterred, Creffield married Maud Hurt the very next day before fleeing to Portland. The law finally caught up with him when Donna Starr, Burgess's wife, officially filed a complaint of adultery against him, which was a crime at the time. After a manhunt, Creffield was found hiding in a shallow hole dug beneath the Hurt family's house, naked and emaciated. It was later revealed that while O.V. Hurt was at work, Creffield had been crawling out from under the house to conduct orgies with his female followers, who had been sneaking him food. He was finally tried, found guilty of adultery, and sentenced to two years in prison.

Creffield was released from prison after serving only seventeen months, and he immediately set out to reassemble his flock. His followers, who had been released from the state insane asylum where their families had committed them, remained as devoted as ever. He gathered them once more, this time with the goal of establishing a "New Eden" on the Oregon coast. After a failed murder attempt by the enraged Lewis Hartley, whose gun misfired five times — an event Creffield touted as proof of his divine protection — he abandoned the majority of his followers in a remote cave at Cummins Creek, telling them to wait for his return while he and Maud went to Seattle.

But Creffield's day of reckoning was at hand. George Mitchell, the brother of Donna and Esther, had been consumed with rage for months over the abuse his sisters had endured, tracked Creffield to Seattle. On May 7, 1906, as Creffield and Maud walked down the sidewalk, George stepped out from the shadows, raised his pistol, and fired a single bullet into the back of the prophet's head, killing him instantly. George Mitchell sat calmly on the curb, smoked a cigar, and waited for the police. The public, believing the murder to be entirely justified, rallied behind him, raising thousands for his defense. At his trial, after O.V. Hurt gave a heart-wrenching testimony about the destruction of his family, the jury returned a verdict of not guilty.

The saga, however, was far from over. The followers who had been left in the cave were discovered nearly a month later, starving and delusional, still waiting for their leader to return. When they learned of his death, they were devastated, but none took it harder than Esther Mitchell. A few days after her brother's acquittal, as George prepared to board a train, Esther approached him at the station. After a brief farewell, she pulled out a gun and shot her brother in the head, killing him in the exact same manner he had killed Creffield. During the investigation, it was discovered that Maud Hurt had conspired with Esther to commit the murder. Before she could be tried, Maud committed suicide in her jail cell by swallowing strychnine. Esther was found to be insane and was sent to a psychiatric hospital. A few years after her release, still haunted by her past, she took her own life in the same way, poisoning herself with strychnine at the age of twenty-six. And so, the reign of the Holy Rollers ended not with a divine resurrection, but with a trail of broken lives and a series of tragic, violent deaths, a testament to how one charismatic stranger could walk into a quiet town and tear it apart from the inside out.

16

THE GHOST IN THE SKY

The day before Thanksgiving, 1971, was a time of hurried motion across the United States, a great annual convergence of families preparing for the holiday. Airports were filled with the low hum of routine travel, a backdrop of gate announcements, rolling luggage, and brief farewells. At the airport in Portland, Oregon, the rhythm was no different. Travelers checked in, milled about the gates, and waited for their calls to board Northwest Orient Flight 305, a short, thirty-minute commuter hop to Seattle, Washington. Among the anonymous faces in the terminal was a man who approached the ticket counter and gave the name Dan Cooper. He was described as being in his mid-forties, with a slim build, and he was dressed in the unremarkable attire of a traveling businessman: a dark suit, a white shirt, a narrow black tie, and a pair of mirrored sunglasses that concealed his eyes. He paid twenty dollars in cash for his one-way ticket, a transaction so ordinary that it would have been forgotten by the end of the day.

In an era before the stringent security protocols that would later define air travel, boarding a domestic flight was a simple, almost casual act. There were no metal detectors to walk through, no baggage X-rays, no mandatory identification checks, no nothing. It was entirely possible to walk onto a commercial airliner carrying anything one could conceal in a briefcase or coat pocket, just as Dan Cooper did. He found his assigned seat, 18C, at the very back of the Boeing 727, lit a Raleigh cigarette, and flagged down a flight attendant named Florence Schaffner to order a drink: a bourbon and Seven Up on the rocks. He settled into his seat, a quiet and solitary figure, just another passenger on a short flight home for the holidays.

The plane took off on schedule, climbing into the gray, overcast sky of the Pacific Northwest. As it ascended, Cooper leaned forward slightly and handed the folded note to Florence Schaffner. She initially dismissed the gesture, assuming it was the clumsy, unsolicited advance of a lonely businessman — a phone number, perhaps, or a forward invitation. She slipped the note into her purse without a glance. But Cooper leaned closer, his voice low but firm. "Miss," he said, "you'd better look at that note. I have a bomb." The quiet insistence in his tone, a stark contrast to the casual atmosphere of the cabin, cut through her professional composure. She retrieved the note and read the neatly printed words. They were stark and direct, stating that he had a bomb in his briefcase and that he wanted her to sit beside him.

Schaffner felt a surge of cold disbelief, but one look at the man's impassive face told her this was not a joke. She asked to see the device, and Cooper obliged, cracking open his attaché case just enough for her to glimpse a terrifying arrangement of wires, red-colored sticks that resembled dynamite, and a large battery. It was undeniably a bomb. He calmly closed the case and laid out his terms. He held the bare ends of two wires, making it clear that all he needed to do was touch them together to detonate the device and tear the plane from the sky. The hijacking of Flight 305 had begun.

Following Cooper's instructions, Schaffner walked to the front of the plane and discreetly informed the captain. The message was relayed from the cockpit to the control tower in Seattle, a calm but urgent transmission that set in motion a massive, multi-agency response. Northwest Orient, the FBI, and local law enforcement were all alerted. On the ground, officials scrambled to react, but inside the pressurized cabin, Dan Cooper remained a picture of composure. He sipped his bourbon, smoked his cigarettes, and politely but firmly reiterated his demands to the flight crew.

He wanted $200,000 (about $1.6 million today), delivered in a knapsack. And he wanted four parachutes: two primary back chutes and two reserve front chutes. The flight attendants, now including a second stewardess named Tina Mucklow who had become the primary liaison with Cooper, carried his handwritten demands to the captain. Cooper, ever meticulous, would later ask for these notes to be returned to him, ensuring he left as little evidence as possible.

Northwest Orient's president, Donald Nyrop, immediately authorized full cooperation. There would be no attempt to challenge the hijacker; the lives of the passengers and crew were the only priority. In Seattle, FBI agents rushed to Seafirst Bank to procure the ransom money. They gathered 10,000 individual twenty-dollar bills, meticulously photographing each one to create a record of their pre-recorded serial numbers. The cash was stuffed into a bank bag and placed inside a knapsack as instructed. Meanwhile, authorities at McChord Air Force Base were tasked with providing the parachutes.

While the complex logistics unfolded on the ground, Flight 305 circled Puget Sound for two hours, burning fuel to ensure a safe landing weight. During this time, Cooper's demeanor never wavered. He was calm, even gentlemanly, engaging in polite conversation with Tina Mucklow. He paid for his drink and even offered to tip her. His apparent lack of agitation was unnerving. He seemed entirely in control of the situation, a man executing a well-rehearsed plan.

Finally, the plane landed at Seattle-Tacoma Airport. Cooper directed the pilots to taxi to a remote, isolated section of the runway, far from the main terminal and shrouded in darkness and rain. There, a single airline employee drove out to the aircraft with the knapsack of money and the parachutes. The exchange was tense but smooth. The items were handed over through the plane's galley door, and once Cooper had confirmed the contents, he made good on his word. He allowed all thirty-six passengers and two of the flight attendants, including a visibly relieved Florence Schaffner, to get off the plane. The passengers, who had remained entirely oblivious to the life-threatening drama unfolding just a few rows behind them, walked off into the rainy Seattle night, believing they had been delayed by a simple mechanical issue.

The flight crew — the pilot, co-pilot, flight engineer, and Tina Mucklow — remained as hostages. Once the plane was refueled, Cooper gave his new, highly specific flight plan. He instructed the pilots to fly towards Mexico City, a destination the captain immediately explained was impossible. They did not have enough fuel for such a long journey. The captain suggested Reno or Phoenix as alternatives. "Reno's nice," Cooper replied casually. "Let's go to Reno."

He then issued a precise set of flight instructions that were both bizarre and dangerous. The plane was to fly at a low altitude of 10,000 feet (about 3,000 meters high), with the landing gear and wing flaps extended down, a configuration that would limit its speed to a sluggish 200 miles per hour (about 322 kilometers per hour). The cabin was to remain unpressurized. The autopilot was set to a low-altitude flight path known as Victor 23. This unusual setup suggested to the crew that Cooper knew exactly what he was doing; he was creating the ideal conditions for a low-speed, low-altitude parachute jump. To enforce these conditions, two Air Force F-106 fighter jets were scrambled to shadow the airliner, but they struggled to maintain the slow speed and were forced to repeatedly circle the hijacked plane rather than follow it closely.

With the flight underway, Cooper ordered Tina Mucklow to go to the cockpit and remain there with the rest of the crew, ensuring he would be alone in the main cabin. As she left, she saw him tying something around his waist; she assumed he was securing the heavy bag of money to his body. A short time later, at approximately 8:13 p.m., a warning light illuminated in the cockpit, indicating that the aft stairway door at the rear of the plane had been opened. The Boeing 727 was one of the only commercial aircraft with such a feature, and in 1971, there was no mechanism — known as a Cooper Vane — to prevent it from being deployed in mid-air. The crew felt a sudden, distinct change in the cabin pressure. The pilot got on the intercom. There was no answer. The man who called himself Dan Cooper had jumped from the plane, disappearing with his money and parachutes into the raging, black storm of the Pacific Northwest night. He was never seen or heard from again.

When the plane landed safely in Reno, it was met by a swarm of FBI agents and law enforcement, who were stunned to find the hijacker gone.

An immediate and thorough search of the aircraft yielded what little evidence Cooper had left behind: the black clip-on tie and mother-of-pearl tie pin, eight Raleigh cigarette butts, and two of the four parachutes he had requested — one primary chute and one reserve chute that had been partially opened, perhaps for him to inspect its components. The bomb, the briefcase, and the ransom notes had all vanished with him.

Working with the crew's detailed statements, the FBI quickly produced a composite sketch of the suspect. Aviation experts at Boeing, using the plane's known flight path and the precise moment the cabin pressure changed, calculated a probable drop zone. Factoring in the severe weather and strong westerly winds, they designated a vast, twenty-eight square mile (about seventy-two square kilometers) search area of dense, rugged wilderness near Ariel, Washington. On Thanksgiving morning, one of the largest and most intensive manhunts in American history began. For weeks, hundreds of FBI agents, National Guardsmen, and military personnel, assisted by helicopters and spotter planes, combed the dense forests and remote farmland. They found nothing — no parachute, no money, no knapsack, and no body. It was as if Dan Cooper had been swallowed whole by the wilderness.

The story of the audacious crime captured the public's imagination, and the media quickly elevated the hijacker to the status of a living legend. In an early wire report, a journalist mistakenly referred to him as "D.B. Cooper," and despite immediate corrections, the catchier, more alliterative name stuck, forever cementing his place in American folklore. In the turbulent context of the early 1970s, an era defined by the Vietnam War, civil rights protests, and a deep-seated distrust of authority, many people saw Cooper not as a violent criminal, but as a modern-day pirate, a cool and clever gentleman thief who had executed a daring plan and gotten away with it.

For nearly a decade, the case remained a frustrating cold file for the FBI. Then, in February 1980, what seemed like a major breakthrough occurred. An eight-year old boy named Brian Ingram was digging a fire pit in the sand while on a family picnic on the banks of the Columbia River, at a spot called Tena Bar. His hands uncovered three decaying, tightly bound bundles of cash, the rubber bands still clinging to the moldy bills. His family turned the money over to the FBI, where the serial numbers were checked against the ransom list. It was a definitive match. The discovery of $5,800 of Cooper's money, however, only deepened the mystery. The location was more than twenty miles (about thirty-two kilometers) from the originally designated drop zone, and in the opposite direction of the prevailing winds on the night of the jump. Geologists added another layer of confusion, determining that the money was found above a layer of sand that had been dredged from the riverbed in 1974, meaning the cash must have arrived on the riverbank at least three years after the hijacking. This led many to speculate that Cooper himself, alive and well, had returned to bury it, but an extensive excavation of the area yielded no further clues.

Years turned into decades, and the case file swelled with over a thousand suspects, but none could ever be definitively linked to the crime. The legend of D.B. Cooper only grew, celebrated annually in Ariel, Washington, with a party in his honor. In July 2016, after forty-five years of fruitless investigation, the FBI officially announced it was closing its active investigation into the Cooper case, citing a need to redirect resources to other priorities. The case was now officially cold, left to a dedicated subculture of citizen sleuths, amateur detectives, and independent researchers who refused to let the mystery die.

It was one of these groups, led by scientist Tom Kaye, that began to apply modern forensic technology to the old evidence, a process that systematically dismantled the myth of the expert hijacker. Using a powerful electron microscope, Kaye's team analyzed the clip-on tie Cooper left behind. They discovered thousands of particles of rare elements, including pure titanium, cerium, and strontium sulfide. In 1971, this specific combination was exceptionally rare, strongly suggesting that Cooper may have been an engineer, a manager, or a chemist at a high-tech manufacturing firm, possibly in the then-booming aerospace industry. Boeing, in fact, was a major user of these materials at the time.

This new scientific lens also reframed Cooper's actions on the plane. The long-held assumption that he was an experienced parachutist was challenged. A true professional, investigators now argued, would have made very different choices. He would have specified large-denomination bills to reduce the weight and bulk of the ransom; instead, the twenty-dollar bills made the money bag a cumbersome twenty-three pounds (about ten kilograms). He chose the inferior of the two primary parachutes provided, an older military-style chute known as an NB-8, which was uncomfortable, difficult to deploy, and non-maneuverable. He also jumped on a stormy night, into freezing, 200-mile-per-hour (about 322 kilometers per hours) winds, wearing a business suit and loafers with no helmet, goggles, or gloves. His claim that he didn't need instructions for the parachutes, once seen as a sign of expertise, was reinterpreted as the bluff and bravado of a desperate amateur.

The most crucial piece of the puzzle remained the recovered money. Tom Kaye and his team revisited the discovery site and, using modern GPS and archival photographs, made a pivotal discovery: the 1974 dredging had stopped 150 feet (about forty-five meters) short of where the money was found. This meant the original FBI conclusion was wrong; the money had not been buried after 1974 but had likely been deposited on the riverbank naturally, within months of the jump. With this new timeline, the only logical way for the money to have traveled over twenty miles (about thirty-two kilometers) from the drop zone was by water.

Kaye's team constructed the first truly comprehensive theory of Cooper's final moments. Reviewing the flight path, they determined that at the moment of the jump, the plane was directly over the Lewis River. Given the non-maneuverable NB-8 parachute, the powerful westerly winds would have carried Cooper directly into the frigid, turbulent waters of either the Lewis River or the vast Lake Merwin. Hitting the near-freezing water, laden with a twenty-three-pound (about ten kilograms) bag of money and likely entangled in his parachute harness, his chances of survival would have been almost zero. Hypothermia would have set in within minutes. His body, along with the money, would have been carried down the fast-running river toward its confluence with the Columbia. This explained how the money got into the river system, but not how it ended up upstream on a sandbar. Kaye proposed a final, grim possibility. At the time, the Columbia River was a busy shipping lane. It's plausible that Cooper's body and the money bag became snagged on a ship's propeller and were carried upstream. The violent motion could have ripped the bag open, spilling some of the contents, which then washed ashore before being covered by sand. As for Cooper's body, the powerful currents of the Columbia would have likely pulled it out into the Pacific Ocean within days, where it would be lost forever.

This scientific account suggests the legendary outlaw did not survive to enjoy his spoils on a beach in Mexico, but instead died a cold and lonely death that very night. Yet, while evidence points to his death, the mystery of his identity remains. Over the decades, a number of compelling suspects have been proposed. There was Robert Rackstraw, a Vietnam veteran with extensive paratrooper and explosives training, championed by a team of private investigators but long-cleared by the FBI. There was L.D. Cooper, whose niece came forward claiming he was the hijacker. And there was Walter R. Peca, another military veteran identified through linguistic analysis of a potential hijacker letter. Each suspect came with a tantalizing narrative, but never any definitive proof. The scientific evidence strongly suggests a tragic and solitary end, but without a body, without a confession, the case remains suspended in uncertainty. The official file may be closed, but the legend of the man who hijacked an airplane and leaped into history endures, a ghost in the American sky.

17

THE COMMANDO KILLER

He sat calmly on the minibus, a man on the run who had evaded capture for three years. But his distinctive features, the kind that are impossible to disguise, had given him away. Another passenger, glancing from the news on his phone to the man's face, had made the connection. The man, a brilliant and methodical killer, understood immediately that the chase was over. He stopped the vehicle, crossed the road, and boarded another bus heading in the opposite direction, a final, desperate gambit, but it was too late. The witness had seen it all, noting the new license plate and alerting the authorities. When the police pulled the minibus over and boarded, the man offered no resistance. He simply stood and surrendered. "I won't run anymore. I'm very tired," he said. "Okay, I am Atalay Filiz."

The capture of Atalay Filiz marked the end of a manhunt that had gripped Turkey, a story involving international disappearances, meticulously planned executions, and a killer who possessed a chilling combination of high intelligence and profound social detachment. He was a classic organized killer, a type more commonly associated with European or American case files, a rarity in the annals of Turkish crime. Unlike many killers who emerged from the margins of society, Filiz was a product of privilege and promise, a man whose intellectual gifts made his descent into brutal violence all the more terrifying.

Atalay Filiz was born in 1986 in Balıkesir, Bandırma, the son of a staff colonel and military pilot who later became a captain for Turkish Airlines. From a young age, it was clear that Atalay was exceptionally intelligent, but this brilliance was coupled with a deeply asocial and cold personality. His teachers would later describe him as a student who was remarkably successful yet unsettlingly unpredictable, a boy from whom you could "never know what he would do or what would become of him." He harbored a persistent dream of living abroad, of escaping the confines of his own culture for something different.

His academic prowess was undeniable. He gained admission to Istanbul's Galatasaray High School, one of the most prestigious and difficult-to-enter schools in the country, and graduated with honors. He finished third in his class. Yet, when it came time for the university entrance exams in 2005, he made a deliberate choice that baffled those who knew his capabilities. He intentionally answered questions incorrectly, sabotaging his own results. His goal was not a Turkish university; it was France. With his father's financial support, he enrolled in a biology program at the University of Paris-Sud.

It was in France that Atalay's life took the first of its dark turns. His father, through his military connections, arranged for him to connect with Göktuğ Demirarslan, the son of a close army friend who was also studying in Paris. The young men became roommates, sharing a house. It was during this period that Atalay, who had reportedly never had a girlfriend in high school, experienced his first real romance. He met a Russian exchange student named Olga Seregina and quickly became infatuated, his affection spiraling into a powerful obsession. The social circle was completed when Olga's friend, another Russian student named Elena Radchikova, began dating Göktuğ. For a time, the couples lived a seemingly normal student life.

As time passed, Atalay's obsession with Olga intensified. They even vacationed together with his family in Fethiye, Turkey, in August 2011. But the relationship was fraught with conflict, and Olga told her friends that she wanted to end it but couldn't. Soon after, Olga vanished. On December 16, 2011, she was working as a babysitter for a family in Paris. She had asked her employers for permission to leave, explaining that a friend of her boyfriend, Atalay, had arrived and she needed to meet him. She walked out of the house and was never seen again. Open-source records later confirmed that Atalay Filiz was in France on a ten-day military leave at the time of her disappearance. For investigators and those who knew the depths of his obsession, the conclusion was inescapable: Olga was his first victim, a trial run for the murders that would follow.

With Olga gone, Atalay returned to Turkey, but his focus had shifted with a predatory intensity. His obsession transferred directly onto Elena. He began to relentlessly pursue her, bombarding her with messages and emails. His advances were firmly rejected; Elena was in a committed relationship with his roommate and friend, Göktuğ. He even tried to sabotage their relationship, falsely telling Elena he had a video of Göktuğ cheating on her. For a man with Atalay's narcissistic and controlling personality, this rejection was an intolerable wound. His infatuation curdled into a lethal combination of jealousy and rage. The primary motive for the double murder was now clear: if he could not have Elena, then no one could, especially not his friend. This motive was compounded by a growing paranoia. He became convinced that Göktuğ and Elena not only suspected him of murdering Olga but were also sharing their suspicions with others, threatening to expose him.

His response was not one of panic, but of cold, methodical planning. He purchased an old, inconspicuous beige Fiat 131 car with a Kütahya license plate and drove to Ankara, where the couple now lived. In a move that demonstrated both his technical foresight and his fatal arrogance, he planted a tracking device in Göktuğ's car. It was a simple old-school mobile phone rigged to a charger and hidden in the gasoline vent pipe, but the SIM card inside was registered in his own name — a crucial mistake that would later unravel his entire scheme.

His initial plan to ambush them was thwarted when the couple left for a fifteen-day vacation in Antalya. Atalay waited patiently. When the tracking device signaled that their car was finally on the move, he put his plan back into motion. On the evening of September 16, 2013, in a housing complex in Ankara's Eryaman district, he prepared his disguise.

He put on women's clothes and a headscarf, and used a makeup kit to alter his appearance, transforming himself to avoid recognition. Armed with a hunting rifle he had legally purchased after obtaining a license by feigning mental health issues, he set up an ambush among the trees. As Göktuğ Demirarslan and Elena Radchikova approached their home, he opened fire at close range, shooting them both. As they lay wounded on the ground, he approached and fired a single, final shot into each of their heads, splattering skull fragments as far as ten feet (about three meters) away.

The double murder initially stumped the police. There were few eyewitnesses, and the killer had vanished. The investigation dragged on for months until relatives of Demirarslan took his car for maintenance and workers discovered the hidden tracking device. The SIM card provided the police with their first solid lead: the name Atalay Filiz. They cross-referenced this with security footage from the area, which showed a beige Fiat 131 car repeatedly circling the neighborhood in the days leading up to the murders, a car that was conspicuously absent after the killings. The vehicle was eventually found abandoned in Istanbul a month later. Inside, police discovered the makeup kits and hair dye alongside a grim collection of tools that could be used for dismemberment: an excavator, a shovel, various saws, screwdrivers, ropes, and surgical materials. An arrest warrant was issued on October 31, 2013, but Atalay was already gone.

For the next three years, from 2013 to 2016, Atalay Filiz was a ghost. Evidence suggested he had spent time in Portugal in January 2014, where his mother and sister were also staying in a different hotel. Throughout his time as a fugitive, he demonstrated remarkable adaptability and foresight. He used a series of false identities, most notably Furkan Altın, and relied on his intelligence and language skills to survive. He worked odd, low-profile jobs that paid in cash — as a waiter, a porter in a cafe, and in a kebab shop — allowing him to avoid creating a digital or financial footprint. He was known to carry large amounts of cash, including Euros, to facilitate quick movements. During this period, he also dedicated himself to honing his survival skills, meticulously studying commando training manuals and reading everything he could find about how to live off the land. In a warehouse he had rented, police later found murder novels, films, and CDs of the show *Dexter*. This was not the behavior of a man simply hiding; it was the preparation of a man who intended to remain a fugitive indefinitely.

In 2016, he surfaced in Tuzla, a district of Istanbul. Using his alias, he got a job as a waiter at a tea garden owned by a history teacher, Fatma Kayıkçı, and her husband. They even rented him a nearby apartment. He lived a quiet, unassuming life, though his behavior was odd; he avoided cameras, used back roads, and didn't respond to his fake name unless it was shouted. For a time, it seemed he had successfully buried his past.

But Fatma Kayıkçı was an observant and intelligent woman. She began to grow suspicious of her quiet tenant. She had a sense that he was entering her home and going through her belongings. A meticulous person by nature, she began to measure the exact placement of objects on her desk, noting their positions millimetrically. When she returned, she found that they had been moved, confirming that her tenant had been searching through her personal information.

One evening, while watching a television news program, a segment re-airing the story of the 2013 Ankara murders came on. As the fugitive's face was shown on the screen, Fatma froze. She recognized the man wanted for a brutal double homicide as her tenant, "Furkan." On May 27, 2016, as he was leaving his apartment, she confronted him at the door. "What's up, Atalay?" she asked. That simple question, born of courage and recognition, was a death sentence.

Realizing his cover was blown, Atalay's survival instincts took over. He began stalking his landlady. The next day, he ambushed her, stabbing her eleven times. In a final act of brutality designed to conceal his crime, he dismembered her body, packed the remains into a large suitcase, and abandoned it in a nearby wooded area.

With the discovery of Fatma's body, Atalay was once again a fugitive, now the subject of a nationwide manhunt. He fled to a place where he believed he was most equipped to survive: the forest. Putting his years of self-study into practice, he spent about a week living in a national park near Izmir, surviving by eating frogs and insects and using gels to ward off flies. But eventually, he grew tired of hiding and decided to make another escape, likely planning to flee the country for good.

It was this final escape attempt that led to his downfall. He made his way to Izmir, where he boarded a minibus. It was there that a fellow passenger, scrolling through the news on his phone, recognized the most wanted man in Turkey sitting just a few feet away. The chase that followed was brief, ending with his calm and almost resigned surrender. When he was captured, he was carrying a survival kit of his own making: two hunting knives, pepper spray, four fake IDs, three fake driver's licenses, fourteen credit cards, a fake French citizenship certificate, and a large amount of cash in both Turkish Lira and Euros. He also had a bizarre list of pornographic film actresses, mostly from France, with their addresses written on a kebab order slip.

The aftermath of his capture was as sensational as the manhunt itself. While in custody, a police officer took a "selfie" with a smiling Atalay Filiz. The photograph was leaked to the media and caused a national outcry. Citizens were disgusted that an officer would pose cheerfully with a notorious triple murderer, and the incident led to an internal investigation, becoming an infamous footnote in the case's history.

In custody, Atalay Filiz remained a chilling enigma. He denied any involvement in the disappearance of Olga. For the murders of Göktuğ Demirarslan, Elena Radchikova, and Fatma Kayıkçı, he was tried and received three separate aggravated life sentences. He was found to be mentally sound and fully culpable for his crimes. He expressed no remorse for his actions. He was the classic organized killer: highly intelligent, meticulous in his planning, and able to maintain a facade of normalcy while harboring a profoundly violent nature. He displayed all the hallmarks of a narcissistic personality, with a complete lack of empathy and an unshakeable belief in his own superiority.

He did, however, offer a twisted justification for the murder of Göktuğ Demirarslan. He claimed that Göktuğ was a member of the FETÖ terrorist organization, an entity widely reviled in Turkey. In his warped logic, he was not a murderer but a patriot carrying out the will of the people. "By killing him," he stated, "I actually fulfilled something the Turkish citizens wanted." He offered no such rationale for the murder of

Elena, whose only crime was rejecting him, or for Fatma Kayıkçı, whose only crime was discovering the truth. His was a mind that operated on a logic entirely its own, a cold and calculating intelligence devoid of humanity, forever marked by the chilling contradictions of a brilliant student and a brutal killer.

18

A CHILD'S DEATH SENTENCE

The words from the judge were a formal declaration, a procedural stamp on a life already derailed. But for the fifteen-year-old boy at the center of it, the reality of the sentence took time to land. It was in the sterile, echoing corridors of the classification unit that the abstract legal term — *life without parole* — began to take on a terrifying, concrete shape. A deputy called out to his colleagues, his voice a mixture of bureaucratic process and disbelief. "Man, we got a juvenile down here and he was just sentenced to life."

Suddenly, Kenneth Young was no longer just another young offender in the juvenile wing. His sentence made him an anomaly, a liability. He was abruptly pulled from the juvenile section and thrown into confinement, the isolation a direct consequence of the legal weight now attached to his name. "You can't come out of confinement because of your sentencing," they told him.

He was still a child, trying to grasp a concept that confounds many adults: a life sentence. The words did not register; they felt detached from his reality. Officials delivered the decision with blunt finality, informing him that he would not be going home and that his life would end behind bars. The idea seemed impossible, and he pushed it away. Everything had happened too quickly — one day he was a fifteen-year-old moving through society, the next he was removed from it and told he would never return. He had been condemned to die in a Florida prison for crimes committed at fourteen even though across the four robberies that led to his sentences, no one had been killed.

Before the robberies, before the courtroom and the life sentence, there was a boy trying to navigate a world that had offered him very little stability. Kenneth Young grew up in a low-income area of Tampa, Florida, an environment where the lines between survival and crime were often blurred. His father passed away when he was too young to form lasting memories, leaving a void that was never filled. The dominant force in his young life was his mother, Stephanie, a woman he loved deeply but who was locked in a decades-long battle with crack cocaine addiction.

His childhood was a chaotic rotation of neglect and fleeting moments of care. There were times when his mother would lock him and his sister in a room and disappear for days on end. As a young boy, Kenneth would get on his bicycle and ride through the neighborhood, pedaling toward the known drug houses, trying to find his mother and pull her away. He would plead with her to come home, to take a shower, to eat. On other occasions, when her addiction overwhelmed her ability to parent, his grandparents would step in, taking the children into their home and providing a semblance of order.

At school, teachers saw a kid who wasn't aggressive or foul-mouthed, but who was clearly struggling. He would show up late, tell jokes, and flash wads of cash that a twelve-year-old had no business possessing. The money and the beeper were constant problems, symbols of a street life that was pulling him away from the classroom. One teacher recalled the only time she wrote a disciplinary referral for him. His beeper went off in class, and when she asked for it, he swore at her — an act so out of character that it signaled a deeper turmoil. When the school sent him home and called his mother, she answered and said, "He's with me." He had not gone to the mall or a friend's house; when he was in trouble, he ran to the one person who was both the source of and the solution to his pain.

By the time he was fourteen, he was enmeshed in a world shaped by his mother's addiction. One of her dealers was a twenty-four-year-old man named Jacques Bethea. It was this connection that would irrevocably alter the course of Kenneth's life. According to Kenneth, his mother had stolen drugs from Bethea, and the older man came to collect the debt. He didn't demand it from Stephanie; he turned to her fourteen-year-old son. Bethea threatened to kill his mother if Kenneth didn't help him commit a series of robberies. For a boy who had spent his childhood trying to protect his mother, there was no choice at all.

In the summer of 2000, over a thirty-day period, Kenneth Young and Jacques Bethea embarked on a robbery spree across the Tampa Bay area. The crimes were violent, brazen, and terrifying for the victims. Bethea was the clear leader. He was the one with the gun, a.38 Colt special revolver, and the one who did most of the talking, his voice loud and aggressive as he shoved the weapon in people's faces and forced them to the ground.

At a Comfort Inn, two clerks were working when the pair entered. One clerk, Sandra Christopher, recalled the moment vividly. Two men came through the door, and she knew instantly that something was wrong. One asked for the restroom, and as he walked down the hall, he ran into her coworker, Rosa, who began to scream. Bethea grabbed Rosa, holding her while pointing the gun at Christopher. When Rosa managed to break free and run for help, the men fled.

At another hotel, the scene was even more harrowing. Bethea vaulted over the counter, grabbed a female clerk by her ponytail, and pressed the gun to her head. "Give me the money," he yelled. After she emptied the register, he demanded she open the safe. She told him she couldn't. "If you don't open the safe, I'm going to blow your head off," he screamed. The clerk later testified that Kenneth was not behind the counter with them; he remained in the lobby. At a critical moment, as Bethea's threats escalated, Kenneth appeared at the doorway. "You can't do that," he said. "We have to leave." Enraged, Bethea threw the clerk to the floor, kicked her in the back, and then both he and Kenneth fled.

Kenneth's role, as he later described it, was to act as a scout, to check for surveillance cameras, and to grab the money or valuables once Bethea had control of the scene. He was an active participant, a fact he would later take full responsibility for, but the dynamic was clear: a twenty-four-year-old with a gun and a criminal history was calling the shots, and a fourteen-year-old boy was following his lead. The spree came to an end after a deputy spotted their vehicle, a green Chrysler Sebring. A short chase ended on a dead-end dirt road, where Bethea and Young were arrested. Inside the car, police found the revolver, cash, stolen jewelry, and a VCR containing a tape from one of the robberies.

The trials that followed produced a staggering and deeply unequal outcome. Jacques Bethea, the twenty-four-year-old armed adult who had held a gun to people's heads and threatened to kill them, was given a single life sentence. Kenneth Young, his fourteen-year-old accomplice, was tried and convicted for his role in four separate robberies. The judge handed him four consecutive life sentences without the possibility of parole. For all practical and theoretical purposes, he was condemned to die in prison.

Kenneth Young entered the adult prison system as a "jitterbug," a term used for the youngest, most vulnerable inmates who often feel they have to prove themselves to survive. Yet, in the face of a hopeless sentence, he did something remarkable. Over the next eleven years, in some of Florida's most violent institutions, he maintained a nearly spotless record. He accumulated only one disciplinary report — for not making his bed on a Saturday morning. Because his life sentence made him ineligible for educational or vocational programs — the system saw no point in investing in someone who would never be released — he pursued self-improvement on his own. He earned sixteen certificates, took care of elderly and mentally ill inmates, and worked to become a better person.

While Kenneth was quietly surviving in prison, a legal battle was raging across the country over the constitutionality of sentencing children to die in prison. In 2010, the U.S. Supreme Court delivered a landmark ruling in the case of *Graham v. Florida*. The Court declared that sentencing a juvenile to life without parole for a non-homicide crime was a violation of the Eighth Amendment's ban on "cruel and unusual punishments." The justices argued that "kids are different" — their brains are not fully developed, they are more susceptible to persuasion, and they possess a greater capacity for rehabilitation than adults. The ruling didn't guarantee release, but it mandated that individuals like Kenneth Young be given a "meaningful opportunity to obtain release based on demonstrated maturity and rehabilitation." After exhausting all his appeals, this Supreme Court decision gave Kenneth his first glimmer of hope. He was granted a resentencing hearing.

The hearing became a battleground over the very soul of juvenile justice. The prosecution sought to retry the original case, focusing on the terror the victims had experienced. Sandra Christopher, one of the hotel clerks, testified for the first time, recounting the trauma of having a gun held to her head. "When they say your life flashes before your eyes, it does," she told the court. While she acknowledged Kenneth's desire for release, she added, "I'm not ready to have him walking around where I live, and I'm not moving."

The defense, led by attorney Paolo Annino, argued that the hearing was not about relitigating the past but about assessing the man Kenneth had become. They presented evidence of his exemplary prison record and called a psychologist who testified about the impulsivity and poor judgment inherent in the adolescent brain. Kenneth's mother, Stephanie, took the stand, tearfully reading a letter in which she begged for forgiveness for the role her addiction played in her son's life. "Please, your honor," she pleaded, "help me put my family back together."

Kenneth himself addressed the court, his voice steady and filled with remorse. "First and foremost, your honor, I want to take the time out and say I take full responsibility for my actions and my role in these crimes," he began. "I have lived with regret every day... I am no longer the same person I used to be." He apologized directly to his victims, concluding his statement by quoting the Bible: "When I was a child, I thought as a child, but when I became a man, I put away all childish things."

The prosecution asked the judge for a forty-year sentence, a term that would keep Kenneth in prison until he was around 50 years old. The defense argued for his release, based on the eleven years he had already served and his profound transformation. The decision rested with the judge.

His ruling was a stunning rebuke of the spirit of the *Graham* decision. He acknowledged the many certificates Kenneth had earned but framed them not as evidence of rehabilitation but as proof that "the Department of Corrections and your particular incarceration was appropriate and effective." He dismissed the defense's plea for release with scorn. "If I follow your attorney's request to release you today, I might as well just give you the key to the city, a parade, and dinner at Bern's," he said. "That would be an award, a gift that you will not get from this court. You will not get it, sir, because you do not deserve it."

He acknowledged Kenneth's remorse and rehabilitation but then explicitly stated he would not rely on it. The judge insisted on "personal responsibility and accountability," stating there was no legal basis to blame Jacques Bethea for his conduct. He then sentenced Kenneth Young to 30 years in prison.

The sentence was a crushing blow. It was not life, but it felt like a rejection of everything he had worked for. "I thought that he would probably see that I had shown from the time I was fourteen years old all the way till I'm twenty-six that I have matured," Kenneth said afterward. "I thought that that'll mean something to him. But he just basically told me that it doesn't mean anything."

His legal team immediately saw the flaw in the judge's reasoning. The Supreme Court had mandated that resentencing must provide a "meaningful opportunity" for release based on "demonstrated maturity and rehabilitation." The judge had found that Kenneth was rehabilitated but then explicitly refused to give that finding any weight in his decision. This became the basis for a new appeal. The fight was not over.

By 2019, Kenneth Young had been incarcerated for more than fifteen years. The frightened fourteen-year-old boy handed a life sentence had grown into a man, and his case had become a focal point for a growing number of advocates, lawyers, and law students who viewed his sentence as a stark example of the justice system's capacity for cruelty toward children. The Supreme Court's *Graham v. Florida* decision had cracked open the door to his prison cell, but the path to actually walking through it remained long and fraught with legal obstacles.

Early that year, he was once again brought before a Florida court for a second resentencing hearing. The setting was familiar, but the stakes felt different. This hearing was less about the crimes of the past and more about the man of the present. The central question was whether the child who had made catastrophic mistakes under duress had truly been redeemed by the man he had become.

His defense team laid out the story of his transformation. They presented his immaculate disciplinary record and called witnesses — psychologists and prison staff — who testified to his maturity, his deep remorse, and his role as a mentor to younger inmates. In response, the prosecution re-emphasized the violence of the original robberies and the lasting trauma inflicted upon the victims, arguing that a significant punishment was still warranted. For hours, the courtroom was a theater where the concepts of justice and mercy were weighed against each other.

At the conclusion of the hearing, Kenneth Young was not granted his freedom. The judge handed down a new sentence, one that still stretched for decades into the future. It was not the outcome Kenneth and his supporters had prayed for, but it contained a crucial element of progress: the sentence explicitly acknowledged his youth at the time of the crimes and his proven capacity for change. He was escorted back to prison, not defeated, but determined to hold on to the hope he had fought so hard to reclaim.

For the next two years, his legal team continued their relentless fight. They filed appeals and petitions, pushing the courts to deliver a ruling that would finally give Kenneth a real chance to re-enter the world he had been forced to leave as a boy.

That chance finally came in the summer of 2021. After years of sustained legal pressure and litigation, the Florida courts approved his release. On July 1, 2021, more than two decades after he was first arrested, Kenneth Young walked out of prison, a free man.

Confronted with what many considered an ongoing injustice, Kenneth found a renewed sense of purpose. He had endured years inside some of Florida's harshest prisons and had weathered the devastation of being resentenced. He was no longer the frightened fifteen-year-old who once denied his fate, but a man who recognized a faint, distant light ahead. Once resigned to die behind bars, he now clung to the possibility of something more. He resolved to nurture that glimmer of hope, turning it into strength to keep pushing forward with his case. The boy was gone, but what remained was a man who refused to surrender the one thing the system could never fully take — hope.

19

THE COLT CLAN

In 2012, in a small village in New South Wales, Australia, the ordinary sounds of a school playground — the laughter of children, the rhythmic creak of swings, the scuff of shoes on dirt — were pierced by a comment so disturbing it would unravel a history of secrets buried for nearly half a century. A young girl, playing amongst her friends, casually mentioned that her twelve-year-old sister was pregnant. As if this were not shocking enough, she added a chilling detail: the family did not know which of her brothers was the baby's father. The statement, delivered with a child's unfiltered innocence, betrayed a reality so far outside the bounds of normal society that it was almost incomprehensible. This was not a single, isolated incident of abuse. It was the first loose thread that, when pulled, would unravel the darkest and most deeply entrenched case of generational incest and inbreeding Australia had ever seen, exposing a family clan of nearly 40 people living in a world of their own making, governed by a doctrine of abuse that had been passed down for five generations.

The family was known to the public only by the pseudonym given to them by the courts: the Colt family. It was not their real name, a measure taken to protect the identities of the many children who were victims, and even, controversially, the perpetrators themselves. To the locals in the area around the town of Boroa, the Colts were a mystery. They lived on a large, isolated farm deep in the woods, a property few outsiders were ever permitted to enter. They were known to be standoffish and strange, a reclusive clan that kept to itself. While some of the adults would occasionally leave the property to work odd jobs, for the most part, the family was a self-contained unit, deliberately cut off from the outside world. The community knew there were children on the farm, but they had no idea of the true number, no idea of the squalor they lived in.

The children were the most isolated members of the clan. They were not enrolled in public school until government child services, having noted the family was receiving benefits for a number of children, discovered they were receiving no formal education. Even after they were forced to enroll some of the children, their attendance was extremely spotty. On the rare days they did show up, their appearance was a cause for alarm. They were consistently dirty, their clothes were ragged, and it was clear they were not receiving adequate medical or dental care. They were intellectually and socially far behind their peers, struggling to keep up in the classroom and to interact with other children. Teachers had a strange and unsettling feeling about the family, a sense that something was deeply wrong. Between 2010 and 2012, a concerned individual or group of individuals filed a total of seven "risk of significant harm" reports with the authorities, but for reasons that remain unclear, little was done. It took the unfiltered words of a child on a playground to finally force the hand of the authorities. On July 18, 2012, police and child services officers drove down the long, unpaved road to the Colt farm, prepared to investigate a claim of abuse.

The roots of this nightmare stretched back decades, to a time before the family had even set foot in Australia. The original matriarch and patriarch were given the pseudonyms June and Tim Colt. June was born in 1948, and Tim in 1943. The pattern of inbreeding that would come to define their family had already begun in the generation before them; June's own parents were brother and sister. June and Tim married in 1966 and went on to have seven children of their own: Rhonda, Betty, Sher, Frank, Charlie, Paula, and Martha. Sometime in the 1970s, the entire family left their home in New Zealand and moved to Australia, beginning a nomadic lifestyle that would become a key component of their survival. They moved constantly, from state to state, never staying in one place for too long. This perpetual motion was a defense mechanism, a way to evade the scrutiny of their growing family and peculiar habits.

During this time, Tim Colt cultivated a chillingly effective public facade. He formed a family band, featuring himself, his son Charlie, and his daughter Martha, along with one of his other daughters. They played guitar and mandolin and sang wholesome country love songs, performing at festivals and music halls all across Australia. They gained a small but dedicated following, recorded albums, and even released a collection of love songs. To the outside world, they were a charming, musical, and tight-knit family. This wholesome image was a carefully constructed lie. Behind the scenes, Tim Colt was not just a father and a bandleader; he was the architect of an incestuous cult, and his family was his captive flock.

He had begun sexually abusing his own daughters when they were as young as twelve years old. But his depravity did not stop there. He actively encouraged and normalized sexual activity between his children, brain-washing them from a young age to believe that incest was not only accept-able but expected. He was the unquestioned leader, the patriarch who controlled every aspect of his family's lives, and his doctrine was one of complete sexual freedom within the family, with no boundaries of age or relation. The oldest daughter, Rhonda, went on to have five children; four of them were fathered by her own father, Tim. The youngest daughter, Martha, had six children, most of whom were fathered by her brother, Charlie, though it is believed Tim may have fathered some of them as well. Martha and Charlie eventually began living as a couple, sharing a bed and raising their children — who were also their nieces and nephews — together.

But it was Betty, Tim's second daughter, who was said to be his favorite. She embraced her father's twisted ideology most completely and was groomed to be his successor, the next matriarch of the Colt clan. She went on to have thirteen children, the majority of whom were believed to have been fathered by Tim himself. The cycle was relentless. When one of the girls became pregnant, they were forbidden from seeking prenatal medical care. If a birth in a hospital was unavoidable, they would lie about the identity of the father. The moment they felt the locals in any given town were becoming suspicious, they would pack up their lives and move on, the family band providing the perfect cover for their transient existence.

In 2001, the matriarch, June Colt, died. She was only in her early fifties. Following her death, the family moved again, this time to a very remote area of Western Australia, seeking even greater isolation as their numbers swelled. When Tim Colt, the patriarch and the catalyst for decades of abuse, died in 2009, the cycle did not end. Instead, his children, now adults, worked to perpetuate it. Betty, as planned, ascended to the role of leader. The family purchased the large, secluded plot of land outside of Boroa, a property that was perfect for their needs. It was nestled in a back-woods area, far from the rest of society, a place where no one would even notice they were there. Here, the abuse and inbreeding continued unabated, now entering its fourth and fifth generations. The adult members of the family, themselves victims of their father's horrifying indoctrination, now became the perpetrators, brainwashing their own children to believe that sexual relationships with their parents, siblings, aunts, uncles, and cousins were normal, encouraged, and expected. The youngest members of the clan, many of whom were the products of multiple generations of inbreeding and suffered from severe cognitive delays, were the easiest to manipulate. They were born into a world where they were surrounded by sexual predators, completely cut off from any outside influence that might have told them that their reality was a living nightmare.

When the authorities arrived at the Colt farm that day in July 2012, the first thing that struck them was the sheer squalor of the living conditions. The property housed two travel trailers, a small garden shed, and a larger shed that had been converted into a makeshift dormitory with tents set up inside. Everything was coated in a thick layer of filth. The trailers were filled with dirt, mud, and hazardous materials. Cigarette butts littered the floors, and trash was piled in every corner. In one of the children's beds, officers found a live kangaroo sleeping. The tiny kitchen area was completely unsanitary, with dirt caked onto the cooking surfaces. Windows were broken, and exposed electrical wires snaked across the walls. There was no running water, no toilets, no shower, and no bathtub. The family had been relieving themselves in the woods, and without access to toilet paper, the state of their personal hygiene was unimaginable. A small tub of murky water found in one of the rooms served as the communal hand-washing station. The stench of stale urine and feces was so overpowering that it was almost too much for the case workers to handle.

It was immediately clear that these people had been living in abhorrent, subhuman conditions for years. The decision was made on the spot to remove all the underage children from the farm. A total of twelve children, ranging in age from five to fifteen, were taken into protective custody and placed in foster care while the investigation proceeded. Their physical and mental condition was catastrophic. Nearly all of them had severe, untreated fungal infections and rampant dental decay. They were all underweight and malnourished. They couldn't read or write, and some of them could barely speak coherently. They had never been taught the most basic life skills; they couldn't hold utensils, eating with their hands instead, and some of them didn't even know what toilet paper was. Several of the children walked with a noticeable limp, and one of the boys suffered from severe, untreated psoriasis that covered his skin. Many of them had distinct physical abnormalities, described as low-slung ears and misaligned facial features, the tragic and visible markers of generations of inbreeding. Even the teenagers would soil themselves, having never been properly toilet-trained. The fifteen-year-old, Bobby, was found to be functioning at the level of a kindergartener.

Once in the safety of foster care, the children began to exhibit deeply disturbing behaviors that spoke to the profound sexual trauma they had endured. Even the youngest children were hypersexualized. Cindy, the five-year-old, was caught by her foster parents engaging in sexual acts with herself on multiple occasions, telling them that her older siblings had taught her how. One of the young girls repeatedly tried to kiss her foster father in a sexually inappropriate manner, becoming upset and confused when he stopped her. Two of the boys, nine-year-old Dwayne and twelve-year-old Brian, were caught tying up their eighteen-year-old foster sister, their intentions chillingly unclear. Some of the boys casually told their foster parents that they used to mutilate the genitals of the farm animals for fun, simply because they were bored. During supervised visitations, the siblings would be openly inappropriate with each other, with no sense of shame or understanding that their behavior was wrong.

Slowly, as they began to trust the therapists and caseworkers, the children started to talk. Their stories painted a picture of a world of unrelenting abuse. Seven-year-old Nadia described watching her mother, Martha, and her uncle, Charlie — who was also her biological father — having sex in the tent right next to her. Dwayne explained the family's primary rule for secrecy: they were told to never tell anyone that his father was, in fact, his grandfather, because his mother, Betty, would go to jail if anyone found out. The threat of their mothers being taken away was the tool used to ensure their silence. Thirteen-year-old Kimberly described being forced to perform oral sex on her nine-year-old brother while her eight-year-old cousin watched, and when she told her mother about it, nothing was done. The girls told stories of being tied to trees while they were assaulted by their brothers, cousins, and uncles, sometimes with sticks and other objects. They spoke of running and hiding in the woods in a desperate attempt to escape the constant threat of abuse.

To confirm the children's harrowing testimonies, the court ordered genetic testing on all twelve of the minors who had been removed from the farm. The results were a stark, scientific confirmation of the family's dark secret. Eleven of the twelve children were the products of incest. Some were the children of half-siblings, cousins, or uncles, while others were the product of closely related parents, such as full siblings or a parent and their child. The one child who did not have related parents was five-year-old Cindy, the youngest daughter of Rhonda. Rhonda claimed that Cindy's father was a man she had a brief affair with while working as a fruit picker. It was a telling detail that Cindy, the only child in the group with a diverse genetic background, was also the only one who was well-spoken, developmentally on track, and had no learning disabilities.

The genetic consequences of the Colt family's practices were not just developmental; they were fatal. A two-month-old baby girl named Sally, the daughter of siblings Tammy and Derek, had died from a rare genetic disorder called Zellweger syndrome just before the case broke. This disorder, which is almost always fatal, is autosomal recessive, meaning both parents must carry the same mutated gene for it to occur in their child. The likelihood of this happening increases exponentially in inbred families, where relatives are far more likely to share the same harmful mutations. Sally's death was a direct and tragic result of the generations of inbreeding that had concentrated these lethal genes within the family.

After everything the children had revealed, after the horrifying conditions of the farm had been documented, and after the DNA tests had provided irrefutable proof of years of incest, one would expect the full weight of the justice system to come down on the adult perpetrators. But what followed was a shocking failure of justice. In court, all of the mothers steadfastly denied that even a single case of incest had ever occurred. They concocted elaborate stories, claiming all the children had been conceived by unrelated outsiders — drifters, and in one fanciful tale, a Scandinavian tourist named Sven. They simply could not, or would not, accept the DNA evidence, insisting the court should believe their word over scientific proof.

Because of their complete refusal to acknowledge the truth, the court ruled that the children would be permanently removed from their care. But the criminal consequences were astonishingly light. Of a total of eighty charges — including incest, child sexual abuse, and perjury — brought against eight of the adults in the clan, most were inexplicably dropped. Charlie, one of the worst offenders, who was facing twenty-seven counts, was ultimately acquitted of two counts of raping a minor after a judge cited "inconsistencies" in the young girl's testimony. The women served only brief sentences of one to two years for perjury. The only significant prison time was served by Betty's brother Rodri, who was sentenced to four years for the violent rape of his seventeen-year-old niece, and Betty herself, who was sentenced to twelve months in 2013 after police, using a phone tap, uncovered her plot to kidnap two of her sons from foster care. The same phone tap also recorded her making disturbingly flirtatious and sexual comments to her fifteen-year-old son.

Today, the children who were removed from that farm are protected by a veil of secrecy, their true identities and whereabouts unknown. Many of them are now adults, facing the lifelong task of healing from a childhood of unimaginable trauma. Disturbingly, it seems that some of them have re-established contact with their mothers. Betty Colt's social media accounts show that she is still surrounded by her family, the clan still tightly knit. In one sickeningly ironic post, she shared a photo of herself with two of her relatives, captioned with the words: "Love makes a family." The adults in this case all began as victims of their father, Tim, a man who unfortunately died before he could ever face justice. But at some point, they made a choice not to break the cycle of abuse, but to embrace it, to perpetuate it, and to inflict upon their own children the same horrors they had endured. They knew what they were doing was wrong — the constant moving, the lies about paternity, the threats used to silence the children, all prove it. And for that, the justice system, in its baffling leniency, failed to hold them truly responsible.

20

THE CALL FROM 3:45 AM

Manchester, New Hampshire, holds the title of the state's most bustling city, a place locals have sometimes dubbed "Queen City" or even "Manch Vegas," a nod to illicit gambling operations that dotted its businesses in the 1980s and 90s. It was here, on April 3, 1966, that Lauren Rahn was born. Her early life was shaped by her parents' divorce when she was just an infant, leaving her to be raised by her mother, Judith. Her father remained largely absent from her life. When Lauren was 4, she and Judith relocated to Miami, Florida, but they returned to Manchester six years later. In 1980, they settled into a third floor apartment at 289 Merrimack Street, in the heart of the city. Within months, during her spring break from school, the fourteen-year-old girl would vanish from that apartment, leaving behind a case that remains one of New Hampshire's most curious and tragic unsolved mysteries.

As a student at Parkside Junior High, Lauren was known as a good student and had a fine relationship with her mother. She was drawn to the arts, passionate about singing and dancing, and held a dream of one day becoming an actress in Hollywood. This ambition was fueled by a dissatisfaction with small-town life; she wanted to see what else the world had to offer and seemed to be in a hurry to grow up so she could get out. She spent a significant amount of time with her friends, wandering the streets, and was not against drinking alcohol or smoking marijuana. On occasion, she even spoke of running away to jumpstart her career.

There was a persistent rumor in town about a man who worked at a local corner store, a man who was reportedly interested in young girls and had no issue selling alcohol to minors. In 1980, the legal drinking age was eighteen while Lauren was fourteen. Her aunt, Diane Penal, later summarized the situation, stating that Lauren was not a bad kid or in a dark place; she was an angel who simply "hung around with the wrong people for a while." With Lauren's father out of the picture, Judith was actively involved in the dating scene, navigating several short-lived relationships. Lauren often joined her mother and these men on outings, but Judith always made it clear that her daughter was the most important person in her life. She assured Lauren that she would not hesitate to end any relationship that made her feel uncomfortable.

The day Lauren disappeared was during her April vacation from school. At the time, her mother, Judith, was seeing a professional tennis player who frequently traveled for tournaments. Normally, Lauren would have tagged along, and they would spend the day at the event. On this particular day, however, Lauren asked if she could stay home instead. Judith was reluctant at first, but she recognized her daughter was growing up fast and ultimately allowed it. On April 26, 1980, Judith said goodbye to her daughter, telling her she loved her and to behave before heading out to the tennis match. She planned to be home later that night, having no idea it would be the last time she would ever see Lauren.

With the apartment to herself, Lauren spent part of the day at her favorite convenience store, where she reportedly restocked shelves, possibly in exchange for alcohol. As evening rolled around, she invited two friends over: One male and one female. Their names have never been publicly released, but they can be referred to as Mark and Sarah. The teenagers spent the night hanging out, drinking a six-pack of beer and some wine while watching television. The night seemed to be winding down normally until the early hours of the next morning.

At approximately 12:30 a.m. on April 27, Lauren and Mark were sitting in the living room when they heard voices in the apartment building's hallway. Worried that Judith was returning home and they would be in trouble for drinking, Mark decided to leave. He exited through the apartment's back door, and he later recalled hearing Lauren lock the door behind him as he left. This account was supported by a neighbor, who also reported hearing voices near the apartment around that same time. After Mark was gone, Lauren and Sarah decided to head to bed.

About forty-five minutes later, around 1:15 a.m., Judith returned home with her boyfriend. She immediately sensed that something was wrong. The first unsettling detail was the darkness. All the lights in the hallways of the three floor apartment building were off, which was not normal. When she reached her apartment, she found the second anomaly: the door was unlocked. This was unusual, as she always reminded her daughter to lock it, but she reasoned that Lauren might have forgotten.

Judith checked her daughter's bedroom and saw a figure sleeping in the bed. Assuming it was Lauren, she quietly left the room. Moments later, her boyfriend noticed the third and most bizarre detail: the back door was unlocked and slightly ajar. Judith found this very strange, as they rarely used that door. She decided to wake Lauren to ask why the door had been left open. As she approached the bed, she discovered it was not her daughter at all; it was Lauren's friend, Sarah.

Sarah explained that Lauren had initially been in bed with her, but after a while, she had taken her pillow and blanket to sleep on the couch in the living room. Judith had seen the pillow and blanket on the couch when she first arrived but had assumed Lauren had just been watching a movie and fallen asleep there. When questioned, Sarah, who was intoxicated, could not remember any further details about the night and had no idea where Lauren could be. A frantic inspection of the apartment revealed Lauren's purse, her brand-new sneakers, and a recent birthday gift all still in the living room. None of her other belongings, including her money or clothing, were missing. There were absolutely no signs of a struggle.

Judith's first calls were to family members who lived in town, hoping Lauren might be with them. When those calls led nowhere, she and her boyfriend began to search the neighborhood frantically. With no sign of the girl anywhere, Judith called 911 at 3:45 a.m. to report her daughter missing. When officers responded, there was not an immediate sense of urgency. As is often the case with missing teenagers, police initially suspected Lauren had run away and would return when she was ready. They noted that she had left behind items a runaway would normally take, but at the moment, there was no evidence that any foul play had occurred.

Police did take a statement from Sarah, who informed them of the night's events: she, Lauren, and Mark had been drinking, Mark left, and the girls went to bed. She reiterated that Lauren got up at some point to sleep on the couch, though she offered no explanation for why Lauren might have done this. Investigators also tracked down Mark, whose statement matched Sarah's account. He explained that he left to avoid being caught drinking with underage girls, which suggested he was at least eighteen years old. He was never considered a suspect in the disappearance.

As days passed with no word from Lauren, the police began to revise their runaway theory. They came to believe she had likely left the apartment on her own, perhaps to get more to drink or something to eat, and encountered some form of trouble outside. This theory, however, did not account for the most disturbing discovery of the investigation. Police found that there had been no power outage or blown fuse in the apartment building that night. Someone had physically twisted the light bulbs in every single fixture, on every floor and in every hallway, just enough to extinguish the lights and plunge the building into darkness.

With word of the girl's disappearance hitting the media, a potential lead emerged from a bus company employee who reported selling a ticket to a girl matching Lauren's description on the day she vanished. This was followed by a statement from a bus driver from the same company, who identified Lauren from an old photograph and claimed to have dropped her off in Park Square in Boston. Hope for this lead faded, however, when the driver was shown a more recent photo of Lauren. He expressed doubt, stating he was no longer certain the girl he dropped off was her.

One of the most baffling aspects of the case involved a series of strange phone calls that began right after Lauren vanished. For about a year following the disappearance, Judith began to receive mysterious calls at her home. They always came at the same time: around 3:45 a.m., the exact time she had first called the police to report Lauren missing. The calls were chillingly silent. Each time Judith answered, there was no voice on the other end, only an unsettling silence, as if someone were listening. The calls also increased in frequency during the holiday seasons.

Then, in October 1980, less than six months after Lauren disappeared, Judith discovered strange charges on her phone bill. The records showed calls made from her account, originating from a motel in Santa Monica, California. In that era, calls could be charged to a home phone number by calling the phone company and entering a PIN, a method cheaper than placing a collect call. Someone had a hold of Judith's PIN. Two of the calls had been made to a motel in Santa Ana, California, and one was made to a teen assistance hotline. All three calls were placed in July 1980, approximately three months after Lauren vanished.

Judith had no connections to anyone in California, which made her believe the calls might have been from Lauren. Further investigation into the teen hotline led to a physician in California who ran it, but he claimed to have no knowledge of Lauren or the call. In a strange turn, when contacted by the Center for Missing and Exploited Children five years later, the man's story changed. He was more open about the hotline and admitted that his wife frequently had runaway girls stop by their house for guidance. He allowed for the possibility that one of them may have been from New Hampshire and around Lauren's age, but there was no proof linking Lauren to him.

Frustrated by the stalled investigation, Judith hired a private investigator in 1986. The detective traveled to California to follow up on the phone calls. He reportedly found that the Santa Monica motel from which the calls originated may have been at the center of an adult film industry ring at the time, with an individual supposedly using the location for filming. Despite this, investigators were unable to link this activity to Lauren in any way.

That same year, another odd call was received by a childhood friend of Lauren's named Roger Murcer. Roger was not home, so his mother answered the phone. The woman on the other end identified herself as either "Lori" or "Loren" and claimed to be Roger's ex-girlfriend. The call was brief, and the caller terminated the conversation without providing any more information. The silent calls to Judith's home eventually stopped after she remarried, moved to Florida, and changed her phone number.

Judith has remained firm in her belief that the three calls from California were made by Lauren. She also suspects that one of Lauren's friends knows more than they have said, and perhaps that there was even another person in the apartment that night who Sarah and Mark have chosen to remain silent about.

Over the years, numerous sightings of Lauren were reported, but none were ever confirmed. In 1981, a year after her disappearance, a family member thought they spotted her at a bus station in Boston, but the woman was gone before authorities could follow up. On October 5, 1980, a body was found in Henderson, Nevada, and authorities initially considered it might be Lauren due to a strong resemblance; however, further investigation confirmed it was not a match. The last reported sighting occurred in 1988, in Anchorage, Alaska. The witness claimed to have seen a woman they believed was Lauren, who would have been twenty-two years old, working as a prostitute. Authorities were unable to track down the woman, and the sighting was never confirmed.

In 1985, an unusual turn of events added another layer of unresolved questions to the case: Mark, the male friend who was in the apartment that night, died by suicide. Although he had not been considered a suspect, investigators noted it was a piece of information that could not be ignored, leaving open the possibility that he knew something about what happened to Lauren or was involved and feeling overwhelmed with guilt.

Desperate for a breakthrough, authorities began to examine other similar disappearances in the area. The first name that emerged was Rachel Garden, a fifteen-year-old who disappeared on March 22, 1980, just a month before Lauren, from Newton, New Hampshire, only twenty-five miles away (about forty kilometers). She had been walking home when she vanished, and her case also remains unsolved. An even more striking case occurred on June 8, 1980, just six weeks after Lauren vanished. A twenty-five-year-old woman named Denise Daneault went missing from a bar in Manchester. Denise, who had brown hair and hazel eyes, bore a close resemblance to Lauren. She was a divorced mother of two and lived in an apartment just two blocks away from Lauren and Judith. Like Lauren and Rachel, Denise has never been found.

Decades later, investigators discovered a deeply concerning connection: a suspected serial killer, Terry Rasmussen, who used the alias Bob Evans, had been residing in the Manchester area during that time. Rasmussen, nicknamed the "Chameleon Killer," was eventually linked to the chilling Bear Brook murders, a case involving four female victims found in Bear Brook State Park, just fifteen miles (about twenty-five kilometers) north of Manchester. One of those victims was identified as Rasmussen's own biological daughter. Authorities suspect he may have been involved in up to six other murders or disappearances. However, Terry Rasmussen died in prison in 2010, taking any information he might have had about Lauren Rahn's disappearance to the grave.

In the absence of evidence, police have settled on the simplest theory as the most prevailing one: that Lauren stepped outside her apartment to meet someone, fully intending to return, but was met with foul play. The detail of the loosened lightbulbs, which seems to suggest a planned abduction, is explained away by authorities as an unconnected coincidence — perhaps a prank by another tenant. They argue that an abductor would not go through the trouble of unscrewing all the bulbs, as it would take time and increase the risk of being caught. Others argue it would have the opposite effect, concealing an identity in the darkness.

More than forty-four years later, Lauren Rahn remains missing. The case has grown cold, frozen in the moment a fourteen-year-old girl left her belongings on the floor and vanished from an apartment with an unlocked door. Someone out there undoubtedly holds the information needed to uncover what happened, but as so much time has passed, the silence that began in a darkened hallway continues.

21

THE BONES ON MIDDLE MOUNTAIN

The 911 call came in from Elaine Redwine, her voice tight with a fear that was just beginning to take shape. Her thirteen-year-old son, Dylan Redwine, was visiting his father, Mark Redwine, in Durango, Colorado, for a court-ordered Thanksgiving visit. Dylan had not even been there for a full twenty-four hours, and now his father was texting Elaine to say he couldn't find him. For Elaine, who lived six hours away, that was an impossible scenario. She got in her car and drove, an agonizing journey into a mystery that would consume the state and unravel a dark family secret.

When the first searchers, including Elaine's stepfather, arrived at Mark Redwine's house, the scene was unsettling. The terrain was some of the most rugged in North America, and the temperature that night was predicted to drop below freezing. A missing boy in that environment was a dire emergency. Yet, as searchers scoured the area until 1:00 a.m., Mark Redwine never came outside to help. Instead, at a reasonable hour, he turned off all the lights in his house as if he were going to bed, leaving the search party in the dark.

In the following days, as hundreds of volunteers joined the search, Mark pushed the effort to center on a mountain lake dam about seven miles (about eleven kilometers) from his home. He told everyone that Dylan was a "big fisherman" and that his fishing pole was missing from the house, suggesting his son had wandered off to the dam. Volunteers, including a grieving Elaine, walked the steep, treacherous banks of the lake, finding nothing. Dylan's friends knew the story didn't add up. One friend, Ryan, had been texting with Dylan the night he vanished. Dylan had been excited to see his friends and had made plans to meet Ryan at 6:30 the next morning. He never showed up.

The visit to his father itself had been contentious. Dylan had not wanted to go. It was part of a court-ordered visitation stemming from his parents' bitter divorce. Elaine's mother was sick with cancer, and the family knew it would likely be her last Thanksgiving; Dylan had pleaded to stay with her but the court order was inflexible. Surveillance video from the airport showed a cold reunion, with no hugs or smiles exchanged between father and son. Their first stop was a Walmart, where video showed Dylan and Mark shopping separately. Dylan was seen texting, already making plans to be away from his father.

After stopping for a hamburger, they arrived at Mark's home. Mark would later tell investigators that they had "rough housed" a bit but that no one was hurt. At 9:46 p.m. that night, Dylan Redwine's cell phone stopped working. He was never seen or heard from again.

Suspicion quickly fell on Mark, whose behavior grew increasingly bizarre. He spoke of his son in the past tense at a prayer vigil, saying how much he "loved" and "cared" about the boy, before immediately pivoting to blame Elaine. In his first interview with police, he suggested Elaine was responsible for Dylan's disappearance, claiming his son had run away because of problems with his mother. This theory was flatly rejected by both Elaine and Dylan's older brother, Cory, who insisted Dylan would never run away without contacting one of them.

Two months after Dylan vanished, Elaine and Cory organized a protest outside Mark's house, demanding answers from the last person to see the boy alive. Mark's public response was to accuse his ex-wife of being involved. But investigators were already focused on what was inside Mark's home. During an FBI-assisted search, cadaver dogs alerted to the scent of human remains inside the living room and in the bed of Mark's pickup truck.

Investigators brought Mark in for a polygraph test. Elaine had already taken one and passed; Mark failed miserably. He was found to be deceptive on the key question: "Do you know where Dylan Redwine is?" In the interrogation room, investigators tried to offer him a way out, suggesting it was an accident, that maybe the "rough housing" had gone wrong. They guaranteed they would not arrest him that day if he just led them to Dylan's body. Mark refused, stone-faced, insisting he had no idea where his son was.

Mark Redwine, investigators would learn, had a lot to hide. The true motive, the spark that likely ignited the fatal confrontation, was revealed by Cory. He recounted a trip he and Dylan had taken with Mark years earlier. In a hotel room, the boys had borrowed their father's laptop and discovered a deleted file. What they saw horrified them: pictures of their father, Mark, dressed in women's clothing and a diaper, relieving himself and then cleaning it with his mouth. Cory, sickened, snapped a few photos of the laptop screen with his cell phone.

Cory told Dylan to keep the pictures a secret, but thirteen-year-old Dylan was honest and confrontational. He didn't like to be quieted. In a later argument, Dylan demanded Cory send him the "poop pics," as he called them, to use as a weapon against his father. Cory sent them, an act he would forever regret. Investigators believed this confrontation was the flashpoint. On that last night, Dylan, trapped in a court-ordered visit with a father he despised, had confronted Mark with the one thing that could destroy him.

With Dylan still missing, that secret was about to become public. The family agreed to appear on the *Dr. Phil*, where Elaine and Cory confronted Mark on national television. When Dr. Phil asked Mark if the photos were genuine, Mark launched into a nonsensical, fabricated story. He admitted his face was in the photos but claimed he had fabricated the images himself as part of an outrageous "scheme" to catch Elaine and Cory, whom he *believed* were breaking into his house. He claimed he planted the photos, never intending for them to be seen. For Elaine, watching his convoluted lies and his cold body language, any last shred of hope she had was extinguished. She knew then that Dylan was no longer alive.

The search for Dylan was stalled by the harsh Colorado winter, which closed off the high country around Mark's home. But when the snow melted in the spring of 2013, search teams were finally able to access a rugged area called Middle Mountain Road. The area became a focus after Elaine's stepfather spotted Mark driving down from the mountain early one morning. During a massive, four-day search involving dog handlers, ATVs, and repelling teams, a searcher found a single Nike Air Jordan shoe, a size seven youth, matching the one Dylan was seen wearing in the Walmart surveillance video. The next day, human-remain dogs alerted in the same area, and searchers found two small bones. Then, another searcher looked down and found a long bone. They were Dylan's.

When investigators called Mark to inform him that his son's remains had been found, his response was cold and belligerent. He mockingly told her to pull her head out of a "sociopath ass" and that finding 2% of Dylan's remains does not constitute him being found. He later told her that with only 2% of the body recovered, they could never prove he was murdered. The fishing pole he had insisted was missing — the one that sent hundreds of volunteers on a wild goose chase to the dam — mysteriously reappeared in his garage.

For two more years, the case stalled, as the most critical piece of evidence — the skull — was still missing. Then, in 2015, hikers found a human skull about a mile and a half away from where the other bones had been located. Elaine knew in her heart it was Dylan. With a new, more aggressive district attorney in office, the case was finally brought before a grand jury. The jury returned an indictment for second-degree murder and child abuse resulting in death. Prosecutors did not pursue first-degree murder because they did not have evidence that Mark had planned or premeditated the killing.

Mark Redwine, then working as a trucker in Washington state, was arrested. Video of his arrest showed him looking utterly shocked, telling officers he had "no idea" what the warrant was about. He thought he had gotten away with it.

The trial, nearly nine years after Dylan's disappearance, began in 2021. The prosecution laid out its simple and tragic case: a damaged relationship that turned deadly. To help the jury visualize the crime, prosecutors recreated Mark Redwine's living room in a separate courtroom, allowing them to see the layout and the actual evidence, including the blood found on the couches, floor, and coffee table that was a 100% match to Dylan Redwine.

Elaine testified about her son and her final, unanswered texts to him, including the last one she ever sent: "Dylan please be safe mom is here to come get you." The defense's cross-examination focused heavily on her public accusations, grilling her about comments she'd made on Facebook pages like "Arrest Mark Redwine."

Cory Redwine also testified, describing the horrifying discovery of the photos and the effect it had on his younger brother. In a moment of raw emotion, when asked how he felt about his father, Cory admitted, "I still love him."

The defense argued that the case was thin and built on emotion. They claimed the marks on the skull were consistent with animal damage and that Dylan had likely been attacked by a bear or mountain lion. The prosecution countered, pointing out that predators do not typically move their prey more than a quarter-mile; Dylan's skull was found over a mile from his other remains. Furthermore, it made no sense that a thirteen-year-old boy would be on that remote mountainside in shorts and a t-shirt in the middle of November.

Throughout the graphic testimony, Mark Redwine sat stone-faced, never shedding a tear, never reacting at all, even as witnesses described his son's remains. He opted not to testify. After five weeks, the jury returned its verdict in just six hours: guilty on all counts.

At the sentencing, Dylan's family finally came face to face with the man who had taken his life. His mother, Elaine, spoke through tears, her words filled with grief and disbelief as she imagined her son's final moments — looking up at his father and realizing the truth. Dylan's older brother, Cory, called his little brother a hero, describing him as a brave thirteen-year-old who confronted their father with the honesty and courage Cory wished he himself had shown. When given a chance to speak, Mark Redwine declined, offering no apology or acknowledgment. The judge, condemning his complete lack of remorse and his dismissal of the trial as a "sham," imposed the maximum sentence: forty-eight years in prison.

22

A DEPUTY'S DAUGHTER

In the early hours of May 26, 2012, a young man named Seth Techel was talking to the 911 dispatcher, telling that his wife had been shot. Deputies rushed to the couple's rural trailer home in Agency, Iowa, a small community where everyone knew one another. The first officer on the scene, like most who would arrive that morning, knew the Techels personally. He found Seth outside, visibly distressed, striking a truck and sobbing next to a fence line. Inside, paramedics found twenty-three-year-old Lisa Techel, five months pregnant, dead in her bed from a single gunshot wound.

Seth claimed he was in the shower when the shot rang out. He said he ran to the bedroom to find his wife mortally wounded and then heard a noise in the living room, where he discovered the front door wide open. He saw no one. By his account, an intruder had entered their home, murdered his wife, and vanished without a trace. From the moment the first responders arrived, a primary suspect was identified, but it was not Seth. It was the Techels' mentally unstable neighbor, a man with whom they had been locked in an escalating feud.

To the outside world, Seth and Lisa Techel were the picture of a perfect young couple. They had met as teenagers at a local bowling alley where they both worked, fallen in love, and married in the autumn of 2011. They lived in a small trailer home in Agency, a village of fewer than 1,000 people, and were excitedly awaiting the birth of their baby girl, whom they planned to name Zoe. Their lives were deeply enmeshed in the local law enforcement community. Lisa worked as a jailer in a neighboring county and was a reserve deputy in Wapello County, serving alongside her father, Deputy Todd Caldwell. Seth, who worked a security job, had just been offered a position as a jailer in Wapello and had aspirations of one day joining the sheriff's department himself. On the surface, their future looked bright.

But hidden from the view of their close-knit community was a deeply troubled marriage. In January, just a few months after their wedding, Lisa had discovered text messages between Seth and his co-worker, Rachel McFarland. They had met in late 2011 and quickly began a secret affair. While they were not sleeping together, they had been exchanging sexually charged messages and photos for months. When Lisa confronted him, Seth swore he would end all contact with Rachel. Instead, he purchased a second phone, registered it under the alias "Rick Jones," and continued the illicit correspondence.

On May 25th, the day before the murder, Seth and Lisa were seen around town running errands. They chatted with a worker at their credit union about the pregnancy and had lunch at a local restaurant where a waitress noted their apparent ease and normalcy. All the while, Seth was texting Rachel on his secret phone. The last messages he sent her, after 11:00 p.m. that night, confirmed what Rachel wanted to hear: Seth had told Lisa he wanted a divorce, and she would be packing her things the next day.

According to Seth, the alarm clock in their bedroom went off at 4:30 a.m. on May 26th. He got up to let their dog, Remington, outside while Lisa stayed in bed. He claimed the dog acted as if something was "fishy" outside, though it did not bark. He went back inside, reset the alarm for 5:00 a.m., and lay back down. When the alarm sounded again, he got in the shower. He said he was in there for no more than five minutes when he heard a loud bang from the bedroom. He grabbed a towel, ran into the bedroom, and turned on the light. The dog was cowering in the closet, and Lisa was lying in bed. When he shook her, she moaned faintly. After that he noticed a hole in the covers. He pulled the covers back, and saw a hole in her bra. Just then, he heard a thud from the living room. He grabbed his pistol from the nightstand, ran down the hallway, and found the front door wide open. He ran onto the porch but saw and heard nothing. When he returned to the bedroom, he said Lisa was unresponsive and no longer breathing. That is when he called 911.

The crime scene quickly became chaotic. In addition to the first responders, numerous members of the Wapello County Sheriff's Department arrived, many of whom were friends and colleagues. Within minutes, Lisa's father, Deputy Todd Caldwell, was contacted. He and Lisa's stepmother arrived and were allowed into the trailer to view the tragic scene. Upon seeing his daughter, Deputy Caldwell instantly believed he knew who was responsible, and it was not his son-in-law. Dashcam footage captured him yelling at his colleagues to "go get him now," and the other officers knew exactly who he meant: their neighbor, Brian Tate.

Tate was a disabled veteran diagnosed with paranoid schizophrenia. In the weeks leading up to the murder, the Techels and Tate had been engaged in a bizarre and escalating feud. It began when Seth moved a dead deer from the road into a ditch, and Lisa later saw the deer hide hanging in a tree on Tate's property. The hide was then mysteriously thrown back and forth between the properties. The conflict intensified when Seth encouraged some of his younger friends to vandalize Tate's property, dumping buckets of dog feces on his porch and throwing rocks at his shed. Tate had called the sheriff's department to complain about what he called "acts of terrorism," and the responding officer was none other than Deputy Todd Caldwell. Unaware he was speaking to Lisa's father, Tate told the deputy that the Techels were terrorists. The week of the murder, Lisa had found a deer hide in their driveway, and Seth had later found footprints near his fence line and had to rush their dog to the vet for suspected poisoning.

Prompted by Deputy Caldwell's urgency, officers descended on Brian Tate's home, fully armed and prepared for a violent confrontation. Instead, they found him enjoying a quiet morning with his mother, who insisted he had been sleeping all night. Tate was calm, on his medication, and invited the officers to sit on his porch for a chat.

The investigation at the Techel home proceeded. The Division of Criminal Investigation (DCI) was called in to assist. Deputies confirmed the shower was still wet and dripping. Two cell phones belonging to Seth — his regular one and the "Rick Jones" burner phone — were collected. There were no signs of forced entry or a struggle, and nothing of value had been taken. Seth was not swabbed for gunshot residue, nor was Brian Tate.

That afternoon, Seth agreed to a five-hour interview with DCI agent Chris Thomas. For the first four hours, the interview was non-confrontational, with a local deputy who knew Seth sitting in, likely to put him at ease. Seth repeated his story about the intruder and pointed the finger directly at Brian Tate. However, while the interview was ongoing, other investigators were speaking to Seth's friends. A close friend, Colton Millard, told them that Seth had confided in him about the affair with Rachel McFarland and had even shown him some of the photos she had sent. This information was immediately relayed to Agent Thomas, and the tone of the interrogation shifted. The interview ended abruptly when Seth's father secured him a lawyer, but the damage was done. The DCI was now convinced that Seth Techel had a lot to hide.

The murder weapon was found the next day. A Mossberg model 500 shotgun was lying in plain view in some tall grass about 90 feet (about 30 meters) from the trailer's front door. The gun belonged to Seth's former roommate, who had left it in the trailer when he moved out. Crucially, Seth had omitted this specific shotgun from the list of firearms he had provided to the DCI. The gun was found with one fired round jammed in the chamber, something friends of Seth said had never happened when they had fired it, suggesting it may have been last used by someone unfamiliar with the weapon.

The evidence against Seth was now overwhelming. He had a powerful motive: he wanted out of his marriage to be with Rachel McFarland but feared a divorce would alienate his influential father-in-law and destroy his burgeoning law enforcement career. His texts to Rachel, particularly the "just give me two more weeks" message and the lie about telling Lisa he wanted a divorce, were damning. Six weeks after the murder, Seth Techel was arrested and charged with first-degree murder and the non-consensual termination of a human pregnancy.

Seth's first trial began in February 2013. The prosecution laid out what they saw as a simple motive of love and lust. Rachel McFarland testified about the affair, and a co-worker testified that after a heated phone call with Lisa, Seth had remarked that "it would be easier if she was in Iraq and died." The defense argued that Brian Tate, who had passed away in the months prior to the trial, was the real killer. They criticized the police for their "tunnel vision" and for overlooking potential evidence at the scene. After four agonizing days of deliberation, the jury came back deadlocked, split ten to two in favor of a guilty verdict. A mistrial was declared.

A second trial was held two months later in a different county. No new evidence or arguments were presented. The result was the same: another hung jury, this time split nine to three for guilty. Again, a mistrial was declared.

Days before a third trial was set to begin, the defense made a bombshell discovery. Lisa's cell phone, which had been collected at the scene, had never been properly examined by investigators. When its contents were finally accessed in May 2014, they revealed a stunning secret: Lisa had also been having an affair. Text messages between her and a co-worker, Jason Tennis, showed an affair that had begun before her marriage to Seth and had apparently continued after. Tennis, when questioned, initially lied about the affair but later admitted to it, claiming their sexual relationship had ended a couple of months before the murder.

The third trial commenced just three days later, with the defense's request for a continuance denied. They now argued there were three potential suspects besides Seth: Brian Tate, Rachel's spurned ex-boyfriend, and now Jason Tennis. Tennis denied any involvement in the murder, and his wife provided an alibi. A rushed DNA analysis showed he was not the father of Lisa's unborn child and did not match the DNA found on a cigarette butt in the Techels' driveway. This time, the new evidence was not enough to sway the jury. After three trials, they were finally able to reach a unanimous decision: Seth Techel was found guilty on both counts.

In September 2014, after years of legal battles, Lisa's family was given the opportunity to deliver their victim impact statements. Her father, Todd Caldwell, once a staunch supporter of his son-in-law, now faced him as his daughter's killer. He recounted how Seth had told his wife that he had looked into Lisa's eyes as she took her last breath. "I have nightmares about that," he told the court. "And in my nightmares, I always wake up and wonder if Lisa was thinking, 'I need my dad.'" Seth Techel received the maximum sentence: life in prison without the possibility of parole, plus an additional twenty-five years. His subsequent appeals were all unsuccessful, bringing the tragic case to a final, definitive close.

23

THE CIPHER THAT FBI COULDN'T SOLVE

On June 30, 1999, the St. Charles County Sheriff's Department in Missouri received a call just before 1:00 p.m. A woman driving near Route 367, close to the town of West Alton about twenty miles (about thirty-two kilometers) outside St. Louis had spotted something unusual in a cornfield — a dark mound lying among the crops. As she got closer, the shape resolved into a human body, already in an advanced state of decomposition under the sweltering summer heat.

Investigators heading to the scene had a grim sense of foreboding. This particular stretch of road was remote, isolated, and had a history. Just four years earlier, in 1995, the body of an alleged sex worker had been found nearby, riddled with bullets. It was known locally as a dumping ground, a place where inconvenient problems could be quietly disposed of. This new discovery was likely another homicide.

They found the body lying face down: a slim, 5'6" (about 167 centimeters) African-American man, dressed in filthy Lee blue jeans and a stained white t-shirt. The scene offered few immediate clues. There was no murder weapon, no signs of a struggle, and given the location, no witnesses. The state of decomposition suggested the body had been lying there for weeks, exposed to the elements. It was sheer luck, investigators realized, that he had been found at all before nature reclaimed him entirely.

A search of the body yielded no identification, only an emergency room ticket and two crumbled pieces of paper tucked into a front pocket. These papers would become the central, enduring mystery of the case. They were covered in what initially looked like random scribbles — a chaotic jumble of letters and numbers spread across more than 30 lines of text. At first glance, it seemed like meaningless gibberish.

But closer inspection revealed a deliberate structure. Certain combinations of letters repeated consistently. Some sections were circled, almost like items checked off a list. Numbers — 74, 75, 194 — appeared sporadically. Parentheses grouped specific letter combinations. It wasn't random; it was structured, complex, and seemingly coded. Someone, investigators believed, had invested considerable time and thought into creating these notes. The question was, who? And more importantly, what did they mean?

With no other leads, the body was sent for forensic identification. The advanced decomposition made identification difficult, but miraculously, the fingertips were preserved well enough to yield a match in the police database. The victim was Ricky McCormick, a forty-one-year-old local gas station employee. To the investigators' surprise, no one had reported him missing.

Armed with a name, detectives began trying to piece together Ricky's final days, hoping to understand how he ended up dead in a remote cornfield so far from his St. Louis home. They spoke to his girlfriend, Sandra. She confirmed Ricky didn't own a car and relied on hitchhiking or public transport. This squared with the lack of any vehicle at the scene or registered in his name. But the cornfield was twenty miles (about thirty-two kilometers) from his home, in an area with no public transportation routes. How had he gotten there?

Ricky's family painted a picture of a man plagued by chronic health problems — heart and lung issues, severe asthma, persistent chest pain — exacerbated by heavy smoking and an alarming consumption of caffeinated drinks, sometimes up to twenty a day. Could he have walked?

Given his poor health, a six hour plus trek through the Missouri heat seemed improbable. Yet, his family insisted it wasn't impossible, suggesting he might have collapsed and died from the strain. The more likely scenario, however, was homicide: someone had brought him there, dumped his body, and disappeared.

The emergency room ticket found in his pocket provided a starting point for a timeline. Hospital records showed Ricky had walked into Barnes-Jewish Hospital on June 22nd, complaining of chest pains and shortness of breath. He was admitted for observation and released two days later, on June 24th. After leaving the hospital, he visited his favorite aunt, Gloria. She told police their conversation was unusually brief and guarded. He revealed little about what was going on in his life and declined her offer of a ride, leaving after only an hour.

The very next day, June 25th, Ricky went to another emergency room, this time complaining of breathing difficulties after mowing grass. Doctors diagnosed an asthma flare-up and released him the same evening. But according to Aunt Gloria, he apparently didn't go home, instead spending the night in the hospital waiting room. Was it his health, or was something else going on? Gloria began to suspect he might have known his life was in danger and didn't want to involve her.

On June 26th, Ricky called Sandra, telling her he was heading to the gas station for food. It was the last time she ever spoke to him. The last confirmed sighting of Ricky McCormick alive was on June 27th, seen by an employee at the gas station where he worked. His body was found three days later, on June 30th.

The autopsy initially offered little clarity. The advanced state of decomposition, far beyond what would be expected for just three days, confounded the pathologist. The cause of death was officially listed as undetermined. The decomposition mystery, however, had a plausible explanation: a severe heatwave had gripped St. Louis during those exact days. Temperatures soared to 90°F (32°C) with 85% humidity. Forensic experts explained that such extreme heat could drastically accelerate decomposition, altering tissue, obscuring wounds, and allowing insects to rapidly consume evidence. The body could easily look weeks old after only three days under those conditions.

For years, the undetermined cause of death was the official story. However, documents released in 2025 revealed a crucial detail withheld from the public: investigators *had* found a possible cause of death back in 2001. A letter from a detective stated they found a cut to Ricky's throat and believed it was the fatal injury. This shifted the narrative definitively towards homicide. Someone wanted Ricky dead.

Sandra, his girlfriend, provided a potential motive. She told investigators Ricky had been acting strangely, scared and anxious, in the weeks before his death. While he worked at an Amoco gas station, he had also taken on a side job delivering packages, often requiring him to travel out of state via Greyhound bus. Sandra confirmed it was drug trafficking; Ricky would return with large Ziploc bags of marijuana, the size of baseballs. He had made two trips to Florida in 1999. After his last trip to Orlando on June 15th, his fear intensified. When Sandra asked who the drugs belonged to, Ricky told her he was holding them for "Baha," one of the two brothers who ran the gas station. Sandra's immediate thought upon learning of Ricky's death pointed directly at this man: Baha Hamdullah.

The Amoco gas station and the Hamdullah family had a violent history. The original owner, Fawaz Hamdan, was imprisoned in 1994 for murdering his neighbor with a butcher knife. Jumah Hamdullah took over, operating under the alias "David Ratigan," and hired his brother, Baha "Bob" Hamdullah, to help run it. Baha was known to police as a loud, dangerous figure. In 1997, he attempted a drive-by shooting. Nine months later, he opened fire on his other brother, Bajett, who lied to protect him. Later that same month, Baha was arrested for assault after beating a homeless man, Elroy Carr, with a rusty hammer for refusing to leave the gas station property. Two weeks before Baha's trial for that assault, Elroy Carr was mysteriously gunned down. The case against Baha collapsed. Though never proven, police sources were certain Baha had ordered the hit. Detectives knew Baha Hamdullah — with his gang connections, drug use, reported weapon ownership, and history of violence — was a prime suspect in Ricky McCormick's murder.

Investigators identified a second credible suspect: Gregory Lamar Knox, a well-known drug dealer operating in Ricky and Sandra's apartment complex. Knox also had a violent reputation and had been named a suspect in multiple homicides, including murder-for-hire schemes. Crucially, a separate, unrelated investigation had already linked Knox to the Hamdullah brothers. During that investigation, a confidential informant told police Knox was responsible for the murder of a Black man who worked at a gas station on Shaw Avenue, whose body was dumped near West Alton — details that perfectly matched Ricky McCormick's case.

With two strong suspects tied to drug trafficking and violence, investigators set up surveillance. For weeks, they watched the gas station, the Hamdullah brothers' homes, and Gregory Knox's apartment complex. They needed something concrete, anything to link them to Ricky's death or confirm the drug operation. But the surveillance yielded nothing. Without evidence, the suspects were effectively cleared, and the homicide investigation went cold.

The only remaining avenue was the mysterious notes. Digging deeper into Ricky's past, detectives uncovered a complicated history. Family members, excluding his mother Frankie who spoke dismissively of his mental capacity, described him fondly, though they acknowledged he was different. Teachers recalled him telling odd stories and being isolated. He struggled academically, shuffled from grade to grade despite being unable to read or write, and eventually dropped out of high school, functionally illiterate. The only thing he could reliably write was his own name.

However, some family members offered a stunning revelation: as a child, Ricky used to write in code. They described it as meaningless "scribbles" or "chicken scratch" that none of them could ever understand. Could the notes found in his pocket be a continuation, a more developed version, of this childhood habit? It seemed plausible, especially given his illiteracy. This personal code might have been the only way he could write things down.

The St. Charles County Sheriff's Department knew deciphering the notes was beyond their capabilities. In late 2001, the notes landed on the desk of Dan Olsen at the FBI's Cryptanalysis and Racketeering Records Unit (CRRU), the elite cod-breaking division that had tackled everything from Nazi spy codes to the Zodiac Killer's ciphers. Olsen and his team quickly confirmed the notes weren't random; the structure, repeated patterns, and circled sections indicated intent. It was a cipher. The problem was, it was unlike anything they had ever encountered.

The CRRU team tried everything. Manual analysis with graph paper and pencil revealed patterns — the letter 'E' seemed to act as a spacer, certain letter combinations repeated — but no clear system emerged. State-of-the-art cipher-breaking software, updated repeatedly over the years, also failed. Experts from around the world were consulted, but the code remained opaque. Even the American Cryptogram Association, a group of amateur enthusiasts known for cracking codes that stumped professionals, were baffled when presented with the notes at their annual convention. Ricky's cipher operated by unknown rules.

After a decade of fruitless effort, the CRRU faced a choice: give up or go public. In a rare admission of defeat, the FBI released the notes online on March 29, 2011, appealing to the general public for help. "We are really good at what we do," Dan Olsen stated, "but we could use some help with this one." They hoped for a breakthrough similar to the Zodiac case, where a schoolteacher and his wife cracked the first cipher.

The public response was overwhelming. The FBI website crashed under the traffic. Online communities on Reddit, WebSleuths, and Google Groups exploded with theories and attempted solutions. Some speculated it was a simple substitution or transposition cipher. Others proposed more complex systems like the Vigenère or Nihilist ciphers. Frequency analysis showed 'N', 'S', and especially 'E' were common, supporting the 'E' as a spacer theory but contradicting typical cipher patterns where common English letters should be disguised.

Some claimed to have solved it, like one Redditor who used "ACSM" (letters found in the corner of a note) as a keyword, producing a message allegedly from Ricky asking for the notes to be decrypted to explain his death. However, these solutions often lacked methodological rigor, changing systems mid-decryption or removing letters arbitrarily to make them fit, and couldn't be replicated.

The release of more case details in 2012 by the *Riverfront Times*, including Ricky's drug ties and illiteracy, shifted speculation towards shorthand or personalized code. Theories emerged that the notes detailed drug deals, listing dealers, quantities, and money. One plausible theory suggested they were bus routes, as many number combinations (71, 74, 75, etc.) matched actual Metro bus routes in North St. Louis County, and the recurring "NCBE" could stand for North County Bus End/Exchange, a major hub. If true, this could potentially trace Ricky's final journey.

Despite thousands of attempts, no proposed solution has ever been verified by the FBI. The code remains unbroken, joining the mere 1% of ciphers the CRRU examines annually that go unsolved. The most likely explanation is that Ricky, hampered by illiteracy but needing to record information, developed a deeply idiosyncratic system known only to him.

This possibility raises ethical questions. If these are Ricky's private thoughts, should they be publicly dissected, even in pursuit of justice? As Nick Pelling of Cipher Mysteries wrote, reading them might only reveal the struggles of "a poor, illiterate guy," leaving a feeling of "deep sadness."

Ricky McCormick's life was undeniably complex. He faced mental health challenges and lived in difficult circumstances, yet he was also involved in criminal activity and had a conviction for statutory rape. Whether he was a victim exploited by dangerous men like Baha Hamdullah or a willing participant remains unclear. Both Hamdullah and Gregory Knox eventually faced justice for other crimes but were never charged in connection with Ricky's death. Baha Hamdullah was convicted for a separate murder in 2002, had it overturned, was acquitted on retrial, and reportedly moved to Ohio. Gregory Knox served time for drug distribution.

Over twenty-five years after his body was found, the death of Ricky McCormick is still officially unsolved. The two pages of intricate code found in his pocket, perhaps holding the key to his whereabouts, his killer, or simply his private thoughts, remain an impenetrable enigma, a silent testament to a life and death shrouded in mystery.

24

JAZZ MURDERS

The man who has come to be known as "Axeman" moved through New Orleans homes in 1918 and 1919, striking families in their beds, leaving doors chiseled open and household tools abandoned in yards. He was never identified. The city recorded a pattern, not a name: an intruder who preferred night, entered by removing a door panel or taking advantage of a gap, used the victim's own axe or any object at hand, and departed without taking valuables. Some targets survived long enough to describe a dark, looming form. Others were found by relatives or neighbors in rooms where blood had coated walls and floors. The record that remains is a series of scenes — addresses, bodies, instruments close by — that ties the murders together but stops short of proof about the person who carried them out.

The first killing ascribed to the Axeman occurred on May 23, 1918. Joseph and Katherine Maggio, an Italian couple who ran a grocery and lived in the apartment above it, were attacked in their sleep. Entry to the home was forced by chiseling away a lower panel of the door. Their throats were slit; Katherine's wound was so deep that her head was nearly severed. The attacker then used an axe from the couple's own home to inflict additional blows. Evidence was left in plain view. Outside the residence, police recovered the axe, still bloody. A few doors down, they found a razor with blood on it — the likely instrument used to cut the victims' throats. Inside, they noted a pile of blood-soaked clothing the killer had apparently discarded in favor of clean garments before leaving.

Joseph's brothers, Jake and Andrew, lived next door. They did not report hearing the attack. About two hours later, they heard groans and entered their brother's home. Katherine was already dead. Joseph lay beside her, alive but mortally wounded; he died within minutes of their arrival. The proximity of the brothers and the late discovery drew suspicion in the first wave of investigative questions, and attention turned especially to Andrew, who owned a nearby barber shop and had access to razors. An employee recalled Andrew taking a particular razor home days earlier to sharpen it. Police confronted him about the coincidence and about the failure to hear a prolonged assault in the next apartment. Andrew said he had been out celebrating acceptance into the Navy, returned home intoxicated, and slept in a way that masked any noise. He said he woke at 4:30 a.m. for a drink and then heard the groans. With no direct evidence tying him to the crime and plausible explanations for the razor and the missed sounds, he was not charged. Nothing in the apartment suggested theft; drawers were not rifled, and money or goods were not missing. The scene looked like an entry for a single purpose.

A month later, on June 27, 1918, another residence above a business became a crime scene. Louis Bessemer, who owned a bakery, and his mistress, Harriet Lou, slept in the apartment above the shop. A deliveryman arrived in the morning and found the bakery closed when it should have been open. Circling to a back entrance, he noticed a door panel had been chiseled out. Inside the living quarters, he saw blood on walls, floors, and even the ceiling. In the bedroom, Bessemer and Harriet lay in pools of blood, both still alive but severely injured from single axe blows to the head. Police recovered Bessemer's own axe, bloodied, in the bathroom. At the hospital, Bessemer regained enough stability to talk but could only report that he had awakened to a figure leaving the room, too quickly to identify. Harriet's condition was worse. She was in and out of consciousness with extensive trauma and required weeks of treatment.

A worker at Bessemer's bakery, a forty-one-year-old Black man, was arrested without supporting evidence. The timing and his employment status seemed to be the basis for suspicion. No physical link emerged; he was eventually released. While Harriet remained hospitalized, her statements shifted. At one point she described the attacker as a mixed-race man in racist terms. Later she accused Bessemer himself, calling him a German spy and suggesting he had attacked her, then injured himself to cover it. Police searched and found multilingual correspondence in his rooms, which they interpreted as suspicious. He was arrested on that theory, briefly convicted, and then acquitted. Officers who had pursued the espionage angle were demoted. Harriet died after seven weeks of treatment, and Bessemer was again arrested — this time for her murder — held for many months, and finally acquitted. Once more, no one remained in custody for the attack itself.

On August 5, 1918, the pattern reached a new kind of target. Anna Schnieder, eight months pregnant, was found by her husband on their bed, face smashed and scalp lacerated, teeth missing, blood saturating linens. The assault weapon appeared to be her bedside lamp. She had been attacked while sleeping and could recall only a shape leaving the room when she came to. Despite the trauma, she survived, and two days later, she delivered a healthy baby girl. As in earlier attacks, nothing suggested robbery; the intruder had come and gone with no sign of searching or theft.

Five days after Anna's assault, on August 10, Pauline and Mary Brunner woke to sounds from their uncle's room. They found their uncle, Joseph Ramana, bleeding on the floor from head wounds caused by an axe. Some accounts note that the nieces glimpsed a man fleeing — described as dark-skinned, heavyset, dressed in a dark suit with a slouched hat — though the certainty of that description varies among tellings. In the yard, officers recovered an axe. A lower panel of the door had again been chiseled out to gain entry. Ramana, 80 years old, died two days later.

By then, the similarities were clear enough that investigators publicly linked the crimes and increased night patrols. The combination of door panels removed, householder axes used, and the absence of theft suggested one offender or a set of offenders using the same method. The city reacted first with alarm and then with routines designed to make entry harder. Reports of suspicious men with axes spiked and led to false leads. The Axeman waited out the extra police presence for nine months.

The next attack came on March 10, 1919. A neighbor heard screams from the home of the Cortemiglia family and ran inside. Rose Cortemiglia, the mother, staggered into the hall, wounded and clutching her two-year-old daughter, Mary, who had been struck once in the neck and killed. Rose had been struck in the head with an axe. Her husband, Charles, lay collapsed on the floor with similar wounds. Both adults survived after hospital treatment. The child did not. In the aftermath, Rose accused the neighbor who had entered the home that night. He was sixty-nine, ill, and frail. When police dismissed that possibility, she accused his son, Frank, an eighteen-year-old about six feet tall (about 182 centimeters) and 200 pounds (about ninety kilograms). Entry to the house — by removing a small door panel — seemed to rule out a large attacker forcing himself through that gap. Charles denied his wife's story. Nevertheless, police arrested both neighbors. The older man received a life sentence for attempted murder; the younger, accused as the principal assailant, was sentenced to death by hanging. About a year into the proceedings, Charles divorced Rose. Her accusations then collapsed. She recanted, saying neither neighbor had attacked them. The men were released.

Three days after the Cortemiglia assault, a local newspaper received the letter that would define the case in the city's imagination. The author called himself the Axeman, described himself as a spirit and a demon, taunted police, and made a demand: at 12:15 a.m. on an upcoming Tuesday, every home should have jazz music playing. Those who did not "jazz it out," the letter said, would "get the ax." The threat, theatrical as it sounded, had an effect. That night, homes put on records, clubs were packed, bands played continuously, and no attack occurred.

Months passed without a new case. In August 1919, the Axeman reappeared in the record. Steve Barker awoke to a figure standing over his bed and was struck immediately with an axe. He later stumbled to a neighbor's house and collapsed. He could not recall the attack after regaining consciousness. The injuries were severe; accounts say his skull was split. The house showed familiar signs: careful entry, a chiseled door panel, and no theft. Three weeks later, in early September, nineteen-year-old Sarah

Lawmen was assaulted in her sleep by an intruder who entered through an open window rather than a door. Neighbors found her hours later, gravely injured. Teeth were missing; head wounds were extensive. She survived but could not provide a description. An axe lay on the lawn. Because the entry method differed from the door-panel pattern, some considered this event a possible copycat.

The last killing commonly attributed to the Axeman took place on October 27, 1919. Esther Pepitone awoke to noises from the bedroom and, from the doorway, saw two men fleeing. Her husband, Mike, had been struck in the head eighteen times with an axe. He died before police arrived. The scene diverges from the earlier pattern. The number of blows far exceeded previous counts in cases linked to the Axeman, and the presence of two men contrasted with earlier reports of a single shadowed figure. Some sources noted a different tool found at the scene, something used to erect circus tents and a circus was in town at the time. Those details fed the idea that this was not the same offender but an opportunistic killing concealed behind the Axeman's well-known method. Police took note of Esther's composure, which they considered unusually calm.

The Axeman's identity was never established by evidence produced in court. In place of a name, the case accumulated explanations. One centered on motive. Many of the victims were Italian immigrants or Italian Americans, often small business owners — a demographic that had become visible and successful in the city. Police and commentators considered whether the targeting reflected racial or ethnic animus, jealousy, or reprisals disguised as random attacks. Others saw points of overlap with organized crime. The Pepitone case in particular attracted a mafia theory on the logic that two men, a flurry of blows, and an emphatic killing looked like a directed vendetta rather than a serial offender's pattern. The lack of theft across scenes continued to suggest that money or goods were not the goal.

The suspect most often discussed in conversations is Joseph Mumphrey. Two years after Mike Pepitone's death, Esther moved to Los Angeles and remarried a man named Angelo. On the second anniversary of Mike's murder, her second husband disappeared. A man who had done business with Angelo — Mumphrey — came to Esther's door and demanded 500 dollars and her jewelry. Esther retrieved a revolver instead and shot him dead. She told police she believed he had killed her first husband. Background details about Mumphrey made him a plausible focus. He had a long criminal record, was linked to a blackmailing gang that targeted Italians, and had been in and out of prison. The timing of his prison terms lined up in a general way with the period when attacks attributed to the Axeman occurred and when, earlier, Italian business owners were assaulted or murdered in 1910–1912. There were some beatings, some shootings, some undetermined circumstances, all clustered around Italian proprietors during a period of community growth and friction. Mumphrey was free during some of those years and incarcerated from 1912 to 1918, a span that ended just as the Axeman attacks began. However, none of that amounts to proof. It is a timeline and a set of affinities. Esther's identification was never tested in court because the man she pointed to was dead. The Los Angeles shooting removed the possibility of a confession or a trial that could have drawn lines between incidents in two cities.

Another suspect is Jake Bird, arrested in 1947 for a double murder committed with an axe, who then claimed responsibility for many killings across the United States. He had lived in New Orleans as a teenager in 1918–1919. The script notes the practical question raised by the door panels: an adult man of large build would have trouble slipping through the small openings the Axeman created. A teenager might not. That is an observation about size, not about evidence. Bird did not confess to the New Orleans crimes, and no link beyond timing and weapon exists in the account provided.

The question of copycats recurs at the outer edges of the case. Some see the last two events — a window entry in early September and the two men in the Pepitone bedroom in late October — as inconsistent with the core pattern. Others consider whether a single offender could have varied his method when opportunity presented itself. The same kind of debate appears around the 1910–1912 cluster of assaults and killings of Italian business owners. In a city with active organized crime, a period of massive demographic change, and rising resentment toward successful immigrant shopkeepers, some of those attacks could be reprisals, some robberies, some personal disputes, and some the work of a single offender.

The Axeman's presence in the city's history rests on these facts and on the way the case interacted with public fear. The letter promising death to any home that did not play jazz at a specified time may have been a hoax, but it captured the city's attention and produced a measurable response. The open windows shut; door panels were reinforced. Patrols increased and then receded when nothing happened for months. The killings began again and then stopped. Explanations gathered around the gaps, and each explanation reflected a different part of the city's life at the time: ethnic tension, organized crime, opportunistic violence, media theater. Without a confession or physical evidence that could be tied to a suspect, the chapter ends where it began: scenes linked by method and time, a letter that might have been from the offender or might not, arrests that did not hold, and a name — Axeman — that the city gave to an absence.

CONCLUSION

As we close these files, the silence that follows is often the heaviest part of the journey. We have traveled from the deceptive quiet of rural Australia to the crowded streets of Lahore, uncovering the scars left by murder, mystery, and madness. What remains is not just a collection of facts, but a sobering reminder of how easily the thin line between order and chaos can be erased.

The cases we've explored—the unsolved ciphers, the blood-signed contracts, and the shattered trust of global scams—leave us with more than just chills. They force us to confront the reality that the "monsters" of our world are rarely the caricatures we see in films. Often, they are the neighbors who smiled across the fence or the leaders who promised salvation while delivering ruin.

Writing these accounts is an exercise in seeking justice through memory. For the victims of the "Summerfield Six," the "Nanjing University Murder," and the many others mentioned in these pages, their stories deserve to be told with the weight they carry. By acknowledging the darkness, we honor the lives that were caught within it.

As you place this book back on the shelf, you carry these twenty-four stories with you. The world may look slightly different now—a little more mysterious, perhaps a little more fragile. But in understanding the darkness, we are better equipped to value the light.

Thank you for walking this path with me. Sleep well, keep your doors locked, and remember: the truth is always out there, waiting in the files.

A SPECIAL THANK YOU FOR YOUR SUPPORT!

Thank you so much for purchasing this book and joining me on this journey into the shadows. As a token of my appreciation, I'd love to send you a special bonus — the digital versions of two of my best-selling books, completely free:

- 1,144 Random, Interesting & Fun Facts You Need to Know — The Knowledge Encyclopedia to Win Trivia
- Why Do We Say That? 101 Idioms, Phrases, Sayings & Facts! A Brief History on Where They Come From!

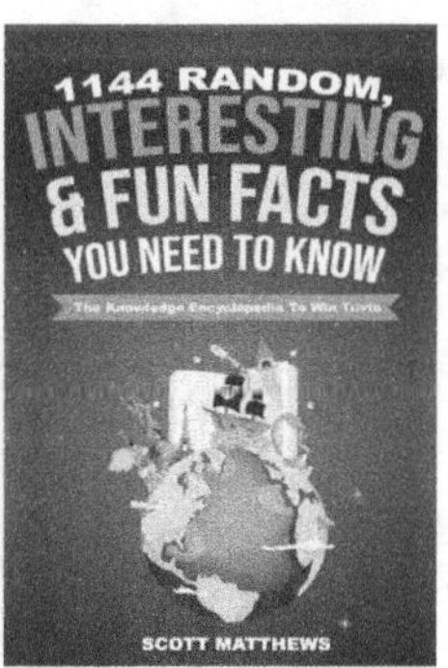

Scan the QR code below and enter your email, and I'll send the files directly to your inbox. Happy reading!

Thank You for Reading!

Thank you for joining me on this journey into the darkest corners of human nature. I hope this exploration of the mysteries behind these cases has challenged your theories and provided a clearer understanding of the search for justice.

If these haunting accounts have left an impression, I would be deeply grateful if you could leave a review on Amazon. Simply scan the QR code below to share your perspective. Reviews are the lifeblood of the true crime community, helping fellow armchair detectives and curious minds find the cases that deserve to be told.

Even a brief reflection makes a significant impact — and I truly appreciate your support in the pursuit of the truth.

See you in the next case file.

Scott

www.ingramcontent.com/pod-product-compliance
Lightning Source LLC
Chambersburg PA
CBHW051518030726
47592CB00006B/2320